DEMONIC ABORTION

DEMONIC ABORTION

A Sobering Commentary
on the Satanic Nature of
the Modern Abortion Industry

By Rev. Thomas J. Euteneuer

Human Life International

© 2010 Human Life International®

Human Life International
4 Family Life Lane
Front Royal, Virginia 22630 USA
www.hli.org

Printed in the United States of America.

ISBN: 978-1-55922-062-0

"A great sign appeared in the sky, a woman clothed with the sun, with the moon under her feet, and on her head a crown of twelve stars. Because she was with child, she wailed aloud in pain as she labored to give birth....Then the dragon stood before the woman about to give birth, ready to devour her child when it should be born....Then war broke out in heaven; Michael and his angels battled against the dragon. Although the dragon and his angels fought back, they were overpowered and lost their place in heaven. The huge dragon, the ancient serpent known as the devil or Satan, the seducer of the whole world, was driven out; he was hurled down to earth and his minions with him...But woe to you, earth and sea, for the devil has come down upon you! His fury knows no limits for he knows his time is short" (Rev 12:1-2, 4, 7-9).

John the Baptist said, "Even now the ax is laid to the root of the tree. Every tree that is not fruitful will be cut down and thrown into the fire. I baptize you in water for the sake of reform, but the one to follow me is more powerful than I. I am not even fit to carry his sandals. He it is who will baptize you in the Holy Spirit and fire. His winnowing fan is in his hand. He will clear the threshing floor and gather his grain into the barn, but the chaff he will burn in unquenchable fire" (Mt 3:11-12).

Contents

Introduction

A Chilean saint, Fr. Alberto Hurtado (d. 1952), often repeated the saying of the famous French priest, Lacordaire, in speaking of the pathway to holiness: "It is proper for the noblest hearts to discover the most urgent need of their epoch and to consecrate themselves to it."[1] Saints always have their feet on the ground and their minds on God or at least trying to discern the Will of God for the transformation of their societies. In this perspective there is little doubt that many of those who strive for holiness *today* will consecrate themselves to the most urgent need of our epoch: namely, putting an end to the wholesale slaughter of the innocents[2] by modern day Herods and Pharaohs. It is to this end that this little book is written. This manual is meant to wake people up and call them to the battle to save lives and souls. The day is far gone and the need has grown increasingly urgent.

Modern American society and, by extension, the rest of the world that is influenced by American politics and culture, is being systematically dismantled before our very eyes by a spiritual force of evil that is not recognized as such. If the devil were to appear to the children of this age as he truly is, in all his ugliness and horror, he would be roundly rejected. So, of course he *doesn't* appear as he truly is. This clever being, it is said, "disguises

---

1 Es propio de los grandes corazones descubrir la necesidad más urgente de su época y consagrarse a ella.

2 In this booklet, the terms "abortion," "abortion industry," "child sacrifice," "culture of death," "slaughter of the innocents" and even "Planned Parenthood" are used generically, almost interchangeably. Where specificity of terms is needed, proper definitions will be spelled out for clarity.

himself as an angel of light" (2 Cor 11:14)[3] and has found count-less illusory costumes in which to conduct his evil, all the while maintaining an appearance of political correctness and accept-ability in polite society. Real Christians don't fall for his deceit, though. We have eyes to see the truth because we are followers of the Truth, and it's time to "consecrate" ourselves to the Truth in a new and bold way.

The idea that the devil is "prowling like a roaring lion looking for someone to devour" (1 Pt 5:8) is not new, but most people are uncomfortable with the idea that the devil could be operating so freely in *their* world. Yet, those of us who have battled the mono-lith of abortion at close quarters have more than an intuition that abortion has a preternatural strength behind it and that it clouds the minds of men and women with a truly demonic perversion of values. The killing of babies as a form of sacrifice to demons has been roundly condemned by God and His Church from the time of the prophets to the present, but sometimes even the ex-ternal face of the dirty business of child sacrifice shows a consis-tency from one generation to the next. For example, the newly-dedicated Planned Parenthood killing center in Houston, Texas (2010) has an architectural design that looks uncannily like an Aztec pyramid, where the practice of human sacrifices took place for generations. The existence of demons transcends human time, so it is not surprising that the forms of their idolatrous worship should look fairly similar in different cultures and times.

It is a theme of the spiritual life that when an evil is practiced clandestinely for a long period of time, eventually it sheds its in-visible covering and vaunts itself in its hideous garb. Furthermore, God in His Mercy has programmed reality in this way to expose

---

3   Scripture passages taken from *The New American Bible*, Confraternity of Christian Doctrine, Thomas Nelson, Publishers: Nashville, TN, 1970 version, unless otherwise noted.

the nefarious spiritual forces of the underworld for the eyes of all to see. Those who do not reject demons on the basis of faith may then reject them when they see with their own eyes the horrible works of their spiritual hands.

Immense Evil Needs Immense Good to Combat It

A spiritual evil like abortion needs a spiritual force of good to break its power and drive it out of this world. The abortion industry is not just powerful in worldly terms, nor is it just to be understood in its human dimensions. No human being or group of humans on their own can commit such immense atrocities against the human race without a diabolical intelligence and malice giving it power. The scope of the killing, the fervor of abortion's missionaries of death and the seductive force of its ideology transcend the human intellect and will.

Erik Holmberg, in his 1988 documentary, *Massacre of Innocence*,[4] very aptly details the effects of this evil in our world. He titles a section of his film, "The Effects of Child Sacrifice," and lists six frightening results of such unfettered evil in our world. Abortion, he says,

1. Destroys human life;
2. Breaks God's commandments and thereby puts the nation under a curse;
3. Opens the door for and empowers demonic spirits;
4. Binds the practitioners to the demonic spirits (in a blood covenant);
5. Locks women into perpetual travail and sorrow; and
6. Releases powers of deception and witchcraft over people, especially women.

---

4 Erik Holmberg documentary, *Massacre of Innocence*, Reel to Real Ministries, Cleveland, OH: 1988, Part 2.

Holmberg has summarized in a nutshell the nature of the evil that not only causes such destruction in itself but spills over into society in unforeseen and unintended ways.

When all is said and done, it is only the united Christian church, expressed most completely in the authority of the Catholic Church, that has the spiritual resources to *end* the culture of death; a work which it could accomplish *overnight* if it were to ever fully "consecrate itself" to the mission of driving out the demon of child sacrifice from our land. It is painfully evident to any objective observer that the Church has not yet fully taken up this mission. In fact, the lack of unity of Catholics in this country is largely responsible for the prolongation and intensification of the culture of death since the 70s. When Catholic bishops publicly contradict each other on the appropriateness of the nation's Abortionist-in-Chief receiving an honorary degree at a prestigious Catholic university; when 54% of so-called Catholics vote for the most pro-abortion President and elect the most radical Congress in American history; when Catholic doctors prescribe abortifacient birth control, and Catholic hospitals look the other way with a wink and a nod at sterilization and abortion referrals from within their walls; when Catholic women pour into killing centers at the same rate as the pagan generation we are immersed in; when alleged Catholic politicians and public figures use their high-profile positions to aid and abet the prevailing evils or our day—*the Church has clearly become part of the problem instead of being the solution to these evils. The Church at all levels, from the bishops to the people, has clearly failed to understand the demonic nature of the industry that practices its evil right down the street from many Catholic churches. It has also failed to marshal the spiritual resources at its disposal to stop it.*

To this cause, the Church must revitalize its essential identity as Church Militant. All believers in Jesus Christ must "be on guard and pray"[5] in the *spiritual Garden of Gethsemane* in which every child in this land is conceived. Unlike our Master who freely chose to suffer before them, babies have no choice about whether they will be allowed to be born or not, and that Garden of Decision ("choice") could be followed by a remorseless Golgotha administered by the devil and his minions, at any point during all nine months of pregnancy. Unless the disciples of Christ truly awake from their slumber and unite in opposition to the heinous crime, the collective guilt of this industry will fall upon us all as a people, and Jesus will say to us, like He said to the weeping women of Jerusalem on His Way to Calvary, "Do not weep for me. Weep for yourselves and for your children."[6] Catholics will not be held accountable if they fail to stop such an immense evil, but we will receive a withering judgment if we live amidst the evil and do nothing about it. The Medieval poet, Dante Alleghieri (1265-1321), is supposed to have said that "the hottest places of hell are reserved for those who in times of great moral crises maintain their neutrality."[7]

Even though the battle is difficult, we must nevertheless remember the words of St. Paul that, "Despite the increase of sin, grace has far surpassed it."[8] Our Hope in Christ tells us that what we look forward to is an abortion-free society at some point in the future. We are not so naïve as to believe that we could eliminate abortion from the world entirely. That would be tantamount to eliminating sin from men's hearts, but man's heart of darkness is the one thing that has shown itself to be a constant reality

---

5 Mk 14:38

6 Lk 23:28

7 The passage may be an interpretation of a line from Dante's *Divine Comedy*, "Inferno," canto 3, lines 35–42: "This way of wretchedness belongs to the unhappy souls of those who lived without being blamed or applauded."

8 Rom 5:20

throughout all human history. Sin and the works of the devil will be brought to an end on the Day when Christ our King returns "to judge both the living and the dead and the world by fire," as has been traditionally said of Him. Our hope is not in an end to sin in the world of space and time, but in an end to the evil of abortion as an institution and as an acceptable "choice" for men and women anywhere. To this end, Christ will use the hearts that are ready to pray and the hands that are ready to work, and He will, through His Church Militant, drive out the evil of abortion from our midst.

The Church's Spiritual Warfare Against Abortion

Demonic Abortion is a companion to my larger work, *Exorcism and the Church Militant* (henceforth *ECM*), which provides a fuller explanation of the Church's hand-to-hand combat with the devil in the type of spiritual warfare we call exorcism. This work on the spiritual battle against abortion was originally intended to be a chapter of *ECM* but was removed for the sake of keeping *ECM's* focus exclusively on the Church's ritual and practice of exorcism. However, the parallels in the pro-life movement to the expulsion of demons in exorcism are, shall we say, *legion*, and will be explained more fully in the pages of this booklet.

The pro-life movement has an immense amount of resource material on issues and activities related to the effort to restore legal protection to the unborn child, but the present work is not meant to be an analysis of the pro-life issues *per se*. It is rather a spiritual commentary about the abortion industry and its evil spawn, the culture of death. Nor does it intend to analyze pro-life issues from a moral point of view, except indirectly. That is all done effectively in other places and by more capable minds. Here I examine the spiritual power that the Church can marshal in the defense of the most innocent of God's children, the unborn—and their mothers—from abortion. I will also relate this effort to the need to repulse other demonic attacks against the sacred institutions of marriage and the family.

Let us never forget how powerful Christian spiritual strength is when marshaled against the institutionalized power of the devil. I distinctly remember praying a private prayer of exorcism at an abortion mill one day when a very angry woman drove into the parking lot and cursed me while she stomped defiantly into the clinic. I and the sidewalk counselors just continued our prayer, only to see this same woman almost run out of the killing center some short while later with a smile on her face! We wondered what happened. With tears in her eyes, she apologized for her behavior and was particularly sad that she had spoken such vulgar words against a priest. She said that she was very pleased that we had stayed to pray for her and remarked that she could feel the prayer literally "penetrating the walls of the clinic" that day! In fact, she said that the prayer also penetrated her heart. She felt as if *God* had come into her heart. Soon afterward she went across the street to the pregnancy care center and was choosing a name for her baby to whom she ultimately gave birth. The prayer softened her heart, but more importantly, it drove away whatever spirit of anger, fear or hatred was coercing her that day.

May the Lord Jesus enlighten all who read these pages and may the holy angels equip us "against the principalities and powers, the rulers of this world of darkness" (Gal 6:12) in the battle for babies, souls—and, indeed, our very civilization.

Rev. Thomas J. Euteneuer
Human Life International
Divine Mercy Sunday
April 11th, 2010

Figure 1: Temples of Human Sacrifice

Temple of Human
Sacrifice, 1510 AD
Tenochtitlán, Mexico

Temple of Human Sacrifice, 2010 AD
Planned Parenthood, Houston, Texas, USA

Demonic Abortion

1. What is the culture of death?

Pope John Paul II popularized the term "culture of death" in his 1995 encyclical entitled, *Evangelium Vitae,* that is, *The Gospel of Life.* The term "culture of death" refers to any society, region or nation where killing innocent human beings has been legalized and institutionalized. This killing can be legalized through actual legislation, government policies, or through court action to decriminalize the procedure. In many cases, the laws or policies are even rewritten in such a way as to legally define these persons as non-citizens or even non-humans, to further justify the act of killing. In such a case, the killing of innocent children receives not only the sanction of law but also the general agreement of the populace, which signifies its acceptance through active cooperation, apathy or simply silence. Abortion also becomes an economic force in society, since it is fundamentally a lucrative business that benefits an elite few and provides political power to those who promote it.

There are many expressions of the culture of death, varying from society to society, but everywhere it is found, it becomes a devastating force of death. In all cases, the abortion culture kills babies and then, in its wake, kills souls and societies as well. For example, atheistic Communism aimed to systematically destroy the family and used abortion as its instrument to accomplish this purpose. Soviet Russia legalized abortion as early as 1920 and imposed it on all the Soviet bloc countries in the 1950s. Russia is now in a catastrophic demographic freefall, losing more than 800,000 people from its overall population every year, due precisely to the long-term ravages of abortion. Vladimir Putin has referred to this situation as a "national crisis," and although the Russian Duma (parliament) has in recent years restricted the circumstances for getting abortions, these measures are hardly going to be effective in reversing the decline in population after ninety years of baby-killing.

Japan legalized abortion during the tenure of American General Douglas MacArthur after the Second World War, and even at that time it was possible to obtain an abortion through the seventh month of pregnancy. It was considered a "pragmatic" means of reducing population growth. In fact, it was so effective in winnowing several generations of Japanese, that Japan is now *the oldest* nation on earth, with the number of born children declining for twenty-six consecutive years. In the past decade, more than 2,000 Japanese primary and secondary schools have closed, and 60,000 Japanese teachers have lost their jobs due to the absence of children!

2. What is the distinguishing feature of the "worldview" of pro-abortion activists, and where did it come from?

It is important to distinguish between the hard-core pro-abortion proponents—the activists—and the masses of people who just accept it because they naively think it is "necessary" or because they imbibe the rhetoric that abortion is a "woman's right." The activists are people who have become immersed in or even possessed by the ideology of abortion and have become its servants. Demons always need doorways through which to enter people, and seductive systems of unholy ideas, i.e., ideologies, are often the means through which demons capture human minds and, through them, do much evil in this world. One has only to witness the destructive ideologies of the last century to see how much evil that unholy ideas worked into a system can do. Nazism, Communism, Maoism, Darwinism, radical feminism, homosexual activism, even moral relativism are examples of just a few of the pernicious mindsets that have at times taken over the minds of men for great evil. They are the causes of the violent deaths of hundreds of millions of innocent individuals.

A distinguishing feature of the worldview of pro-abortion activists is their ability to see the world in moral terms entirely opposite the Pro-Life/Christian worldview. In many ways their worldview is the complete reversal or denial of authentic Christian and human values. On virtually every single issue related to life and morality, the worldview of the promoters of the culture of death militates against the authentic Christian position.

Figure 2: Worldviews in conflict

Pro-Life/Christian position	Pro-Abortion/Culture of Death position
Jesus Christ is the Lord of life	Worship of no god or worship of pagan deities—secular humanism as a religion
Authentic freedom is always accompanied by duties and responsibilities to others	"Freedom of choice" is an absolute value with no obligations attached to it
Abortion is murder and the violation of the most fundamental human right to life	Abortion is a fundamental human right
Women are partners with men in marriage and society	Women are in competition with men in marriage and society

Figure 2: Worldviews in conflict (continued)

Parents are the rightful teachers of their children about matters of human sexuality	Hedonistic "sexuality educators" and mandatory school-based sex education are in charge of children's education about matters of human sexuality
"Be fruitful and multiply," children and fertility are a blessing; large families are positive	Children and fertility are a burden and oftentimes considered a curse; large families are irresponsible
Contraception is *destructive of* fertility and the marriage covenant	Contraception is *freedom from* fertility
Chastity is a human virtue and fornication is a sin	Promiscuity is a human virtue and chastity is ridiculed
Embryonic stem-cell research is the destruction of human life	Embryonic stem-cell research is advancing science and leading to cures for other human beings
Physician-assisted suicide and euthanasia are murder	Physician-assisted suicide and euthanasia are ways to exercise autonomy in decision-making
Homosexual activity is immoral and homosexual marriage is an illegitimate right	Homosexuality is a lifestyle and should receive endorsement from society as equal to marriage

Figure 2: Worldviews in conflict (continued)

"God made them male and female" and created human nature as determinative of the relationship between them	"Genders" are defined by social convention and are not fixed in nature
Authentic social and political development for the good of societies	Population control to keep down the breeding of those peoples considered "undesirables"

Finally, nothing better shows the radical reversal of the pro-abortion/culture of death mindset than the two maps in Figure 3. The first map shows the world as the abortionists see it: the red-colored areas are places filled with the blood of women who are dying by illegal abortions (according to them). The second map, used by Human Life International in our presentations of the status of abortion around the world, shows the red areas as place filled with the blood of babies that are killed by legal abortion.

Which worldview, pro-life or pro-abortion, gives a more accurate picture of reality, will be determined by history. "Time will prove where wisdom lies" (Mt 11:18).

Figure 3: Blood maps—Pro-Death versus Pro-Life

THE WORLD'S ABORTION LAWS

The map above shows the world as the abortionists see it: the red-colored areas are places filled with the blood of women who are dying by illegal abortions (according to them). The map below, used by Human Life International in our presentations of the status of abortion around the world, shows the red areas as place filled with the blood of babies that are killed by legal abortion.

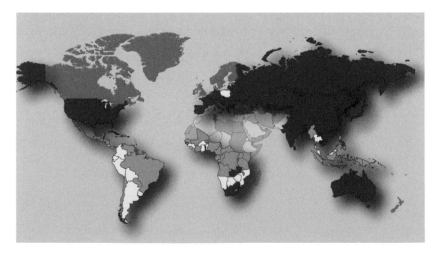

Figure 4: Abortion law summary by continent

Continent	Countries on Continent	Abortion on Demand	Restricted Abortion	Pro-Life Laws
North America	2	2	0	0
Central America	8	1	1	6
Caribbean	25	5	18	2
South America	14	3	6	5
Europe	48	45	1	2
Middle East	16	12	2	2
Africa	56	4	15	37
Asia	50	29	3	18
Oceania	14	4	5	5

3. What is the "unholy trinity"?

The culture of death is not just about the surgical killing of babies. There are other elements that work together with surgical abortion to bring about a culture of death in every country of the world. These elements are the triad that we term the "unholy trinity," since they are always found united in the work of killing life, marriage and family. They are contraception, comprehensive sex education[1] and abortion.

---

1 "Comprehensive sex education," henceforth referred to simply as "sex education," is the Planned Parenthood-style plan of total mental and social indoctrination of children's minds with perverse images and ideas concerning sexuality from kindergarten through 12th grade. It is "comprehensive" in many senses: it covers all topics relating to sexuality, it covers all levels of primary and secondary education, and it seeks to comprehensively alter children's basic system of values, and thereby behaviors, as a means to further the sexual revolution. It is known by counter-intelligence experts as "systematic values (or behavior) modification," and is undoubtedly an effective tool in

Abortion promoters do not go into traditional cultures and try to convince them to start killing their babies. Quite the opposite: oftentimes the abortion-promoters enter disguised as St. Paul describes the devil and his servants, as "angels of the light,"[2] to deceive a culture into thinking that they are *preventing* abortion by promoting contraception as a solution to "unwanted pregnancies." They claim that fewer children will bring greater economic prosperity and that the development of their country is intimately tied to reducing their birth rate. In other words, in overt and subtle ways, they blame the economic poverty of a country on children and stigmatize large families as irresponsible. At times they impose government-ordered limits on childbearing overtly or punish reproduction through other forms of disincentives like social pressure and medical coercion. Along with that, the abortion promoters rarely if ever admit that contraception fails, because they know that when it does, it creates a "need" for abortion as its sinister backup.

These are the standard tactics of the death peddlers. The logic of it was enshrined in a clear opinion of the U.S. Supreme Court in 1992 (*Planned Parenthood v. Casey*) where Justice Sandra Day O'Connor admitted rather frankly:

> Abortion is customarily chosen as an unplanned response to the consequences of unplanned activity or to the failure of conventional birth control…for two decades of economic and social developments, people have organized intimate relationships and made choices that define their views of themselves and their places in society, in reliance on the availability of abortion in the event that contraception should fail.

---

the arsenal of the culture of death. Furthermore, this type of "sex education" has nothing to do with the wholesome Christian program of educating young people in love, self-control and vocational discernment.

2 2 Cor 11:14

If contraception transforms a society's attitudes toward childbearing, programs of sex education in the schools change how the youth of a country behave in matters of human sexuality. Sex education is the systematic *values and behavior modification program* of the culture of death, and it is very effective when it is implemented in the public school systems, far out of sight of the watchful eyes of parents. These programs are not chastity or abstinence education programs according to Christian standards: they are Planned Parenthood-style hedonistic indoctrination about sex. They have a devastating effect on the young: they hook them on birth control, indoctrinate them into alternative lifestyles and open them to the idea that abortion is just another "choice" that they can make when promiscuity gets them into trouble.

Passing from the idea that a child is an "inconvenience" (contraception) to the idea that a child is "irresponsible" (sex education) to the idea that the child is a "problem" or a "crisis" that can only be solved by abortion is the slippery slope that the devil has created in the hearts and minds of people. The corruption of ideas from one to the other has behind it a diabolically clever strategic mind that exploits the innate laziness of human beings in the area of sexuality and literally creates murderers out of mothers and fathers. Patricia Bainbridge, current chairman of Human Life International, regularly says that Planned Parenthood set out decades ago to change the way America thinks about sex—and they were phenomenally successful.

The plan of the "unholy trinity" is to subvert everything that God wants us to consider sacred and is, in essence, "another gospel"[3] entirely opposite of the Gospel of Jesus Christ that the Church upholds and offers to the world for its sanctification.

---

3   Gal 1:6-7

The "unholy trinity" constitutes a demonic assault on humanity, which must be rejected outright by men and women and cast out authoritatively by the Church.

4. In what sense is the promotion of abortion a "conspiracy"?

The term "conspiracy against life" was coined by Pope John Paul II[4] to describe the promotion of abortion on a massive scale. The words of the Holy Father are sobering:

> Humanity today offers us a truly alarming spectacle, if we consider not only how extensively attacks on life are spreading but also their unheard-of numerical proportion, and the fact that they receive widespread and powerful support from a broad consensus on the part of society, from widespread legal approval and the involvement of certain sectors of health-care personnel....[W]ith time the threats against life have not grown weaker. They are taking on vast proportions. They are not only coming from the outside, from the forces of nature or the "Cains" who kill the "Abels"; no, they are *scientifically and systematically programmed threats*.... [W]e are in fact faced by an objective "conspiracy against life," involving even international institutions, engaged in encouraging and carrying out actual campaigns to make contraception, sterilization and abortion widely available. Nor can it be denied that the mass media are often implicated in this conspiracy, by lending credit to that culture which presents recourse to contraception, sterilization, abortion and even euthanasia as a mark of progress and a victory of freedom, while depicting as enemies of freedom and progress those positions which are unreservedly pro-life.

The "conspiracy against life" that Pope John Paul speaks about, thus, has several "alarming" characteristics:

---

4 Pope John Paul II, Encyclical Letter, *Evangelium Vitae*, 17. English translation, Daughters of St. Paul.

- Its attacks against life are exponentially greater than the world has ever known, and they are spreading;

- There is a legal, scientific and social consensus for these attacks;

- The conspiracy is international—a conglomeration of powerful institutions working together;

- It forces its ethic of killing on others in a systematic and scientific way;

- The conspirators are aided and abetted by powerful media propaganda;

- The conspiracy is driven by anti-values or distortions of true values; and

- It identifies those with humane or religious values as enemies.

The Holy Father does not call this "conspiracy against life" demonic, but the way he describes it allows for a deeper reflection on the root causes. In its simplest terms, something so vast, so coordinated and so objectively evil cannot be driven merely by human ingenuity; nor is it driven only by human sinfulness. There is a deeper power to the overall campaign, which suggests a much keener coordinating intelligence than the scheming of human minds. The description indicates a demonic intelligence behind the conspiracy. Fallen angels are perfectly capable of carrying out such a coordinated attack on life through spiritually malicious and weak human beings who hold the reins of worldly power.

5. In what sense is the abortion business demonic?

In secular terms, abortion is fundamentally a business based on a perverse idea of human rights. Ideological concerns about women's "rights" determine the scope of the mission, but money drives it, and we must never forget that if we want to truly understand the power of the abortion industry. Abortion is a commodity that is cleverly marketed to women under the rubric of "free choice" and sold for a price to make huge profits off the deaths of innocents. The abortion industry is a raw killing machine that also generates enormous amounts of cash as it destroys life.

The spiritual dimension of this grisly "business," however, is it's systematizing of *ritual blood sacrifice* to the god of child murder, who, in the Old Testament, is called Moloch. This demon of child sacrifice appears in many forms and cultures through history (Phoenician, Carthaginian, Canaanite, Celtic, Indian, Aztec and others), but it is always the same bloodthirsty beast that demands the killing of children as a form of worship. This demon also seeks public endorsement and ever-new forms of expression to increase his "worship." In some of the ancient images of these evil practices, we see huge drums being used beside the places of sacrifice as the rituals proceed. These drums were used to drown out the screams of the victims who were being sacrificed on their altars and deaden the consciences of those who participated in such evil.[5]

The practice of child sacrifice was condemned as an abomination by the prophets of the Old Testament. Ezekiel said to the people of Israel: "The sons and daughters you had borne me you took and offered as sacrifices to be devoured by them! Was it

---

5 Cited from a sermon by Fr. Frank Pavone at the Legatus Pro-Life Mass in Dana Point, CA, February 5, 2010.

not enough for you to play the harlot? You slaughtered and immolated my children to them, making them pass through fire."[6]

The abortion industry of today offers ritual blood sacrifice to that ancient demon of child sacrifice: it is in every way a demonic religion. It has an infallible dogma ("choice"), a ruling hierarchy (Planned Parenthood), theologians (feminist ideologues), a sacrificing priesthood (abortionists), temples (abortion mills), altars of sacrifice (surgical tables), ritual victims (babies and also women), acolytes and sacristans (clinic workers and technicians), guardian angels (police and escorts), congregations (foundations and private supporters of abortion) and its own version of "grace" which makes everything work (money).

In modern abortion, the "drums" of the ancient rituals are the buckets and containers now used to carry out the obliterated dead bodies of the babies, and the sound of the abortionist's suction machine drowns out the "silent scream" of the innocent one who is sacrificed on the altar of feminism or greed or ideology. The endgame of it all is the burning of the victims as a *holocaust* to the demon. In ancient times, babies were "passed through the fire;" nowadays, the babies sacrificed to Moloch are simply sent out and burned as "medical waste."

The sacrificial victim in this demonic religion is not a brute animal as was offered by the priests of Israel. In abortion, the victim is an innocent human being who is made in the "image and likeness of God" and completely unable to defend himself from the abortionist's aggression or ideology. Furthermore, the baby is sacrificed by his own mother and father who pay an executioner to perform the ritual. This combination of innocence, parental renunciation and ritualized annihilation of the image

---

6   Ez 16:20-21; see also Ez 20:26.31 and 23:37 for even harsher words of condemnation.

of God in human form is the devil's way of blaspheming God, and in this project he can count on the misguided participation of God's own children. The systematic destruction of the human body, which St. Paul calls "the temple of the Holy Spirit,"[7] is also a sacrilege. In short, abortion is a perfect demonic system that offers a perverse form of worship to the devil. If the abortion business is not truly diabolical, nothing is.

Figure 5: The elements of the demonic religion of abortion

Religions of Human Sacrifice	Religion of Abortion
Worship of Moloch	Worship of Moloch
Temples	Free-standing "clinics"
Altars	Abortion surgical tables
Sacrificing Priests	Medical doctors (abortionists)
Ritual blood sacrifice to obtain favors from the demons	Ritual blood sacrifice to obtain profit and political power
Victims are adults of conquered tribes or children	Victims are innocent babies and secondarily women who abort
Religion based upon pagan creeds	Religion based upon dogma of "choice"
Beating of drums drowns out screams	Sound of the suction machine drowns out "silent screams"
Drums used for killing ritual	Drums used to carry dead bodies

---

7   1 Cor 6:19; see also 1 Cor 3:16 and 2 Cor 6:16.

Victims are "passed through the fire"	Victims are burnt as medical waste
Parishioners and congregations	Private donors and foundations
Tribal approval or acquiescence	Public approval or acquiescence

Figure 6: True religion versus false religion

True Religion	The False Religion of Abortion
Male hierarchical priesthood	Feminist hierarchy of Planned Parenthood
Sacraments and sacramentals	Abortion is "holy" and a sacrament (see Appendix A)
Truth	Ideology
Infallible dogmas and doctrines	Infallible dogma of "choice"
Missionary mandate to convert the world	Diabolical mandate to corrupt souls and societies
Acolytes and sacristans	Clinic workers and technicians
Guardian angels	Escorts and police
Grace	Money
Spiritual power of God	Spiritual power of the devil
"I came that they might have life and have it to the full" (Jn 10:10).	The devil is a murderer from the beginning (cf. Jn 8:44; 1 Jn 3:8)

6. What does demonic "ideology" look like?

International abortion *promoters* usually use abstract rhetoric and conventional language to disguise their grisly plans, but for those who *sell* abortion there is no abstraction. They are the grass-roots ideologues who make money off the destruction of babies and the promotion of immorality. Good examples of demonic ideology can be found on the websites of abortion providers and purveyors of the culture of death.

An abortion mill in Pennsylvania,[8] for example, had the following crass description of its abortion "package deals" on its website in recent years, until its sales pitch became too damaging to their reputation, or to their sales, or both. The following excerpt is from a page that was entitled, "How do you want your abortion?" The prices listed are from the early 2000s and most likely have gone up.

> Hi, my name is Jane and I'm going to help you decide what kind of abortion is right for you. First of all, let me say that I'm sorry you are in this situation, but it may help to learn what's available and then decide what's right for you. We have a number of packages available or you can customize an experience that fits with your situation and needs. Let me describe our most frequently requested packages to you.
>
> 1. Economy—This is our most popular package which has been offered since 1973 and enjoyed by several millions of women in the United States. You can expect to be in an abortion facility about 4 hours. Several other clients will be joining you as you learn about the basics of pregnancy termination, birth control, and aftercare. Outpatient surgery is simple, quick, and safe. Personal review of medical history and emotional check-in are available; beverages and

---

8　From the website of Allegheny Reproductive Health Center in Pittsburgh, PA. The website has since been scrubbed of these hideous descriptions.

snacks will be served and a choice of pain relievers is yours, all for a reasonable fee of $350.

2. The Lunch Hour Special—Designed for the busy woman for whom time is more valuable than money. Make your appointment online and submit your personal medical information for review in advance of your appointment. Lab work can be performed at your convenience ahead of time. The physician is kind, quick, and gentle. Some sedatives may not be available in this time frame, but we guarantee service in one hour. $600.

3. The Family Package—This is an important decision in your life and of course you want your loved ones around you!! You can be accompanied through every phase of this process by the person you choose. Counseling is available for all family members and includes training and suggestions for them to participate in your care. Flowers, breakfast in bed, baby-sitting, just tell us what you want and we'll pass it along. We stress support and coping skills before, during, and after your abortion. Choice of abortion pill (additional $100) or surgical abortion. $650.

4. DIY (Do-It-Yourself)—Are you the kind of person who does a lot of research? Someone who knows what you want? Do you want to avoid the hustle bustle—and waiting-time—of a busy clinic? Would you like your abortion in the comfort of your own home? Take a pill today and choose when you bleed anytime in the next three days, safely, completely, in your own home. Full instructions and educational video included and our 24 hour advice line is open to you. Available only in early pregnancy. Some restrictions apply. Like everything else you do, have this experience on your own terms! $550.

5. Deluxe Spa Treatment—Get the luxury and personal attention you deserve!! Check into our special suite at the Jetson Hotel where you will meet with our experienced guide, who will be available to you for your abortion experience. After extensive orientation for you and your partner or family, enjoy a relaxing massage and jacuzzi. Full emotional support is available to you and those close to you, tailored to your needs. A full range of sedatives and pain relievers to choose from make for a pain-free procedure by our experienced and friendly physician. Recover back in your suite and choose from 3 relaxing options—a foot massage, a mud pack facial, or a rebalancing of your shakras by our expert Reiki master. Then, enjoy room service from a 4 star restaurant. Our guide will be available to you to review aftercare and discuss any emotional issues. Full cable and choice of video entertainment available, and enjoy our feather pillow beds for a good night's sleep. $3000.

6. Spiritual Journey—Ending a pregnancy is not just a physical act but also a spiritual process. Meet with our spirit healer and guide a week in advance to plan the ritual journey that will meet your spiritual needs. Native American (Taino clan tradition), Eastern philosophy, nature-inspired (pagan), or custom designed ceremonies are available to you and to the support people who will accompany you on your spirit quest. Or, design your own rituals with the help of our experienced guides. Check-in to our mountain retreat Friday night for a ritual cleansing and spiritual preparation. Have the surgical procedure when you are ready for a separation of paths with the spirit child within you. Miscarriage with medicines and herbs is also available early in pregnancy. A follow-up ritual a year and a day later is included in this package. $5000.

7. Full Emotional Support—Deciding to end a pregnancy may well be the most difficult emotional crisis a woman or couple may face. Our experienced counselor will spend 2 hours with you and a support person of your choice, and your appointment will be scheduled 2-7 days after that. The counselor will explore relationship and identity issues, personal goals, religious and spiritual concerns and offer interactive skill-building to you and your significant other. A choice of 3 self-help books are included with additional suggestions for grief work and emotional aftercare. The procedure will be performed by an experienced and kind physician in privacy, with your choice of pain relievers and sedatives. Or, choose to miscarry with medicine taken at home. ($100 extra.) Two follow-up visits with our licensed and experienced counselors are available one week and one month after the procedure. Consultation by phone with the clergy or spiritual leader from your belief system included, if desired. $1000.

8. Discount Package—A basic "no frills" package is available for those women who don't need ambiance or additional support. No additional sedation is available without additional cost. Licensed physicians perform the safe surgery in less than 5 minutes. Expect delays and waiting time. No support people allowed in counseling or medical areas. If you want to spend the money on something else, this package may work for you, but we encourage you to consult our website for a complete overview of the abortion experience. $250, cash only.

9. Abortions Anonymous—For the woman who wants to tell no one, keep it secret, and have no record of having been there, we offer an anonymous service with private hours. Counseling offered to explore any feelings and potential emotional side-effects. No names taken. $950, cash only.

7. How is abortion related to feminism?

Clearly the evil of abortion was not part of the original "women's rights" movement, as the early feminists all considered abortion an exploitation of women by abusive and irresponsible men. How right they were! The pro-life group, Feminists for Life, exposes the words of so many of the feminist pioneers in their publication, *The American Feminist*: For example, "[Susan B. Anthony's] 1875 speech 'Social Purity,'… specifically discussed abortion and postnatal infanticide—along with rape and prostitution—as male wrongs against women. Anthony argued that laws pertaining to these matters, made and enforced exclusively by men, further victimized women while absolving men of all responsibility." [9]

Modern feminism is both ideologically and organizationally connected with the promotion of the culture of death, promiscuity and evil. A very cursory view of feminist websites will reaffirm this connection. The website of the radical feminist-abortion organization NARAL Pro-Choice America, for example, gives undeniable proof of the "unholy trinity"[10] in full color. NARAL features only four items on the "issues" section of its website: abortion, birth control, sex education and women of color. The explanations of these "issues" read like ideological manuals of the demonic mindset that produces these destructive realities, and

---

9 *Op. cit.*, Vol. 5, No. 1, Spring 1998, p. 19. Feminists for Life regularly features the quotes of the early feminists condemning abortion in no uncertain terms in their publication, *The American Feminist*. In order to conserve space here, I have just cited the quote of the most famous of all the feminist pioneers, Susan B. Anthony, and the website provides ample information for anyone who wishes to study this topic further: http://www.feministsforlife.org/. We must keep in mind, however, that many of the early feminists were against abortion but not against the twin evil of contraception, so it is difficult to hold them up as heroines to our movement. Their witness against abortion simply suffices to show the distance between the founders of the feminist movement and their modern evil progeny.

10 Cf. Question 3 above.

of course youth, vulnerable females and minorities are always the targets of these hateful campaigns! The "unholy trinity" has gained full force against our families mostly due to modern radical feminist activism. Any given feminist group will advocate for the same issues in more or less the same terms, so it is not necessary to multiply references.

8. How does abortion liberalization around the world negatively affect the very women it purports to help?

It is said that every revolution ends up devouring its own, and the feminist revolution is no different. There is indisputable evidence now that abortion targets the very people that feminists were supposed to liberate: namely, females. Female infanticide is the ugly hidden secret of the culture of death. It is estimated that as many as 50 million baby girls have been killed in China alone, and India counts 10 million female deaths by abortion in the last twenty years. A 2005 report by the Geneva Center for the Democratic Control of Armed Forces estimates that abortion and female infanticide accounts for 200 million "missing" women from the world's population.[11] Birthrates of boys to girls are skewed in all regions of the world, including predominantly Catholic Latin America, and are taking an immense human toll on the future of these lands.

Nicholas Eberstadt of the American Enterprise Institute has even noted that the discriminatory killing of girls is showing up in Asian-American birthrates here in the United States. "It can't happen here? Think again: quantitative data and applied statistical reasoning provide us with unavoidable evidence beyond any reasonable doubt that *it is happening here*."[12] The trend is becom-

---

11   http://www.dcaf.ch/women/pb_women_ex_sum.pdf

12   Nicholas Eberstadt, *The Global War Against Baby Girls: An Update*, American Enterprise Institute, 2006.

ing so alarming that even *The Economist* magazine dedicated a whole edition in March of 2010 to the subject of "gendercide." In short, it is hard to see this attack on females as anything other than the revenge of the serpent against the woman. Indeed, the female infanticide phenomenon has been appropriately termed "the slaughter of Eve."[13]

The other perverse effects of abortion on the health and well-being of women have been well-attested to in other places, most especially the Elliot Institute which impressively documents the heightened physical and psychological risks and sequelae of abortion.[14]

9. Who calls abortion a "sacrament"?

Abortion has often been called a "sacrament" by many in the abortion industry and radical feminists. Abortion is also being labeled a "sacrament" in deprecating terms by high-profile abortion opponents[15] in order to point out the "religious" nature and zeal of abortion-promotion. The terminology is explicit and in a sense shocking for anyone who has true religious sensibilities. Labeling abortion a "sacrament" emphasizes the blasphemous nature of what abortionists do in their killing centers. It is important for the pro-life movement to constantly point out the spiritual nature of our struggle against the culture of death, so that we address its evil at the deepest level.

Appendix A contains an extensive list of quotes about abortion as "sacred," "holy," "a blessing," or a "sacrament" by abortion-promoters.

---

13   http://www.nrlc.org/News_and_Views/March06/nv032206.html

14   The marvelous research and Fact Sheets on post-abortion effects can be found at the Elliot Institute's voluminous website at: http://www.afterabortion.org.

15   Ann Coulter, *Godless: The Church of Liberalism*, Crown Forum: New York, 2006.

10. Does the abortion industry use God and religion to promote its killing agenda?

The promoters of abortion must necessarily pervert the God-given voice of conscience in the depths of the human heart in order to get people to justify the decision to kill. True abortion ideologues give a religious, almost messianic, tone to their propaganda and make abortion a type of salvation for women. They know that if they can convince people that God is on their side, the issues of conscience will be less of a barrier to the "choice" for abortion. The manipulation of clergy and the use of religious/spiritual metaphors to get women into their killing centers is part-and-parcel of abortion propaganda.

Many clergy have been co-opted into the anti-human causes of fertility control and the killing of children. Margaret Sanger's "Negro Project," in the early part of the last century, sought to sway the black communities in America to accept the idea of abortion through the use of black ministers who were the community's most influential leaders. In like fashion, Planned Parenthood Federation of America (PPFA) established a "Clergy Advisory Board" in 1994 that claims over 2,000 lay and clerical members. Additionally, every year for the past several years, PPFA has included an "Interfaith Prayer Breakfast" as part of its annual convention![16]

In 2004, PPFA hired the so-called "Rev." Ignacio Castuera as their national "chaplain." Castuera is a Mexican-born United Methodist minister in Los Angeles whose work on behalf of "reproductive choice" makes him the perfect shill for the abortion fanatics who target Hispanic women as a new market. In case anyone wonders whether Castuera might just be mis-

---

16   Neela Banerjee, "The Abortion-Rights Side Invokes God, Too," *The New York Times*, April 3, 2006.

guided or taken advantage of by the abortion industry, Planned Parenthood's press release removes all doubt: "He will play a pivotal role in communicating the theological justification for choice, sexuality, and contraception to the Planned Parenthood community and the general public."[17] In other words, Castuera is nothing more than a clerical hack for promoting abortion among Hispanics.

The target audience for the Religious Coalition for Reproductive Choice (RCRC) is expressed in a simple racist formula: "people of color." They claim to bring "the moral power of religious communities to ensure reproductive choice through education and advocacy." However, their concern about "the poor" should be balanced against their exorbitant salaries and organizational assets:[18] the Coalition's President, Carlton Veazy, draws a salary of $191,568 and pulled $7.5 million in revenues in 2007 for the cause of reducing the Negro population. In fact, the RCRC had an exponential rise in revenues from $1.4 million in 2005 to $7.5 million in 2007.

The most outrageous of the demonic groups using religion to justify abortion is the so-called "Catholics" for a Free Choice (CFFC) group, whose main publication is named after the very thing they wish to kill, *Conscience*. CFFC has a whole series of publications on the theological justification of abortion, one of which is a guide for Catholic women considering abortion that includes a *prayer service* to assuage their consciences from any guilt beforehand![19]

---

17   http://www.plannedparenthood.org/news-articles-press/politics-policy-issues/ignacio-castuera-12492.htm

18   Source: all information on this organization is found on the "Charity Navigator" website: www.charitynavigator.org

19   "You are Not Alone: Information for Catholic Women on the Abortion Decision" (2000). Excerpts from this publication will be quoted in Appendix A.

11. What is the magnitude of abortion's evil?

The killing of innocent babies is intrinsically evil in itself, but it takes on a greater dimension of evil with its growth into a network of systematic extermination, aided and abetted by medical professionals, government leaders and powerful international organizations with coercive economic and legal power.

The statistics-gathering arm of Planned Parenthood, the Guttmacher Institute, estimates that the number of *surgical* abortions each year amounts to somewhere between fifty and fifty-five million dead babies worldwide, which is only a very rough estimate.[20] This number does not take into account the millions killed yearly by chemical means. I imagine that the real number of surgical abortions could be double this estimate, given the fact that countries without legal abortion do not keep statistics about it, and even in the countries that do, there are varying standards of reporting and tracking. In the vast majority of countries, abortions preformed in doctors' private offices are not reported or counted in any official way. Given that abortionists are the ones who have to tell the world how many abortions they commit, they have very little incentive to be truthful about the actual number. In the U.S., abortion is mainly a cash business, and it is recognized that abortionists commonly underreport the number of abortions they commit in order to avoid paying taxes.

One can also get an idea of the evil of the abortion industry— and the evil it spawns—by looking at Human Life International's

---

20   Stanley K. Henshaw, Susheela Singh and Taylor Haas. "The Incidence of Abortion Worldwide." *International Family Planning Perspectives* [Alan Guttmacher Institute] January 1999, Volume 25 Supplement, pages S30 to S38. This number had been steadily increasing for decades, and a simple mathematical extrapolation puts it at 50-55 million annually today.

"pro-choice violence" database.[21] HLI researcher, Dr. Brian
Clowes, has documented over 8,500 acts of violence committed
at the hands of abortionists or other abortion-supporting people,
including: 1,251 homicides and other killings; 157 attempted
murders; 28 arsons and bombings; 904 assaults; 1,908 sex crimes
(including 250 rapes); 106 kidnappings; 422 cases of vandalism;
290 drug-related crimes; and 1,616 medical crimes. And this is
only the tip of the iceberg.

The main purpose of putting together a database of this type
was to highlight the violent nature of the abortion *culture*. The
immensity of the worldwide abortion statistics and the additional violence spawned by it is a small way to document the scope
of this evil, but we must always keep in mind that the killing of
even one innocent baby by abortion is evil and is worth fighting
with all our lives and energies to end definitively, both in law and
in the hearts of all.

12. Why is the culture of death considered *universal* in its scope?

The breathtaking scope of the social engineering planned by
the abortion promoters was summed up perfectly in a 1969
Memorandum by Frederick S. Jaffe,[22] then-Vice President of
Planned Parenthood-World Population. It is one of the most
chilling pieces of demonic shrewdness that has ever come to light.

---

21 Www.pro-choiceviolence.com. This site can also be accessed through the key
words "abortion violence" and "pro-abortion violence" through any internet search
engine.

22 Frederick S. Jaffe (Vice-President of Planned Parenthood - World Population),
Memorandum to Bernard Berelson (President, Population Council) found in
"Activities Relevant to the Study of Population Policy for the U.S." March 3rd, 1969.
A Family Planning Perspectives Special Supplement, Planned Parenthood - World
Population, 810, 7th Avenue, NEW YORK, N.Y. 10019. [*Note:* This article origi-
nally appeared in the October 1970 issue of the Alan Guttmacher Institute's *Family
Planning Perspectives.*]

This document clearly delineated how the "powers that be" would radically alter the landscape of western society. It also shows that the abortion industry's goals have actually been achieved in less than forty short years. The following Memorandum (called the *Jaffe Memo*) was written by Frederick S. Jaffe, VP of Planned Parenthood's World Population bureau to Bernard Berelson, then-President of the Rockefellers' Population Council. It is a verbatim reproduction of the plan he proposed to fundamentally alter the Judeo-Christian view of life, marriage and family. Note that, of the three sections, the first uses the term "universal impact" to describe the desired changes. All bold and italics are mine.

The Jaffe Memo

TABLE 1. Examples of Proposed Measures to Reduce U.S. Fertility, by Universality or Selectivity of Impact

---

[Section 1]

Universal **Impact**

A. Social Constraints

    1. Restructure family:

        a. Postpone or avoid marriage

        b. Alter image of ideal family size

    2. Compulsory education of children

    3. Encourage increased homosexuality

4. *Educate for family limitation*

5. *Fertility control agents in water supply*

6. *Encourage women to work*

[Section 2]

Selective Impact Depending On Socio-Economic Status

A. Economic Deterrents/Incentives

   1. Modify Tax Policies:

      a. Substantial marriage tax

      b. Child Tax

      c. Tax married more than single

      d. Remove parents tax exemption

      e. Additional taxes on parents with more than 1 or 2 children in school

   2. Reduce/eliminate paid maternity leave or benefits

   3. *Reduce/eliminate children's or family allowances*

   4. Bonuses for delayed marriage and greater child-spacing

   5. Pension for women of 45 with less than N children

   6. Eliminate welfare payments after first children

   7. *Chronic depression*

   8. *Require women to work and provide few care facilities*

9. Limit/eliminate public-financed medical care, scholarships, housing, loans and subsidies to families with more than N children

B. Social Controls

1. Compulsory abortion of out-of-wedlock pregnancies

2. *Compulsory sterilization of all who have two children except for a few who would be allowed three*

3. *Confine childbearing to only a limited number of adults*

4. *Stock certificates-type permits for children*

5. Housing policies:
   a. Discouragement of private home ownership
   b. Stop awarding public housing based on family size

[Section 3]

Measures Predicated on Existing Motivation to Prevent Unwanted Pregnancies

A. Payments to encourage sterilization

B. Payments to encourage contraception

C. Payments to encourage abortion

D. *Abortion and sterilization on demand*

E. *Allow certain contraceptives to be distributed non-medically*

F. Improve contraceptive technology

G. Make contraception truly available and accessible to all

H. Improve maternal health, with family planning a core element

[End of memo]

This memo sounds like a summary of the recently-passed healthcare takeover by President Obama and the US Congress. It takes little imagination to see how the goals, so carefully planned out in 1969, have almost universally been achieved, at least in Western society. The ultimate goal of the groups and individuals who share this ideology, not stated in this memo but found abundantly elsewhere,[23] is to take this same plan to the rest of the world. Pope John Paul II called this the "conspiracy against life," as was mentioned above.

13. Is population control considered by the Church to be evil? If so, why?

The Vatican has a long-standing feud with the proponents of population control. The Church's public debate on this issue may be more adequately described as a dramatic clash of worldviews, reaching international proportions. For example, in 1994 the UN Conference on Population and Development in Cairo was dominated by Bill and Hillary Clinton's pro-abortion thugs and attempted to impose abortion on the world as an international human right. In response, Pope John Paul II wrote a sharply-worded letter to Mr. Clinton and another forceful letter to every Head of State *in the world*, objecting to this political maneuver-

---

23   See in particular, the 1974 United States National Security Study Memorandum 200 (NSSM 200, known more commonly as "The Kissinger Report") in which US population control policy was firmly set in stone.

ing as a violation of both justice and basic human rights. In the end, the Holy Father had to ally the Vatican delegation with the Muslim nations because the western (traditionally Christian) nations had all caved into the power politics of population control. This "clash" will only increase in time as socialists, communists and radical feminists take over all western institutions.

The first reason the Church believes population control is evil is because it is nothing more than birth control writ large. The Church knows by long experience that the uninhibited practice of one moral evil always produces another, even greater, evil. In 1968, Pope Paul VI noted in the encyclical *Humane Vitae* the intrinsic connection between the widespread practice of birth control and the practice of coercive population control. He prophesied the advent of the systematic destruction of marriages, families and even whole societies by these coercive means. "Let it be considered," he wrote, "...that a dangerous weapon would thus be placed in the hands of those public authorities who take no heed of moral exigencies.... Who will stop rulers from favoring, from even imposing upon their peoples, if they were to consider it necessary, the method of contraception which they judge to be more efficacious?"[24] All the reasons stated in Question 14 below for the rejection of birth control apply equally to population control.

Secondly, population control violates the sovereignty of nations and inhibits true development. The massive amount of funding given by the rich countries to population programs in the poorer countries usually comes with anti-human conditions attached and skews the provision of funding for a poor country's more primary and pressing needs. Spending millions of dollars on condoms and pills, for example, is an *injustice* since it derails

---

24 Pope Paul VI, cf. *Humanae Vitae*, 17, under the section entitled, "Grave Consequences of Methods of Artificial Birth Control."

needed funds from the most important development works of
building roads, schools, infrastructure and programs for true human development and puts the dollars into the hands of those
who wish to reduce and kill their population. The Holy See has
always lobbied for authentic human and social development over
against inhumane population control programs and deceptive
"reproductive health" measures.[25]

In many senses, then, the Church regards population control
as an injustice, a moral evil and a "structure of sin." In the past
forty years, the Church has issued a prodigious amount of documents, teachings and statements objecting to population control.[26] Although the Church does not use the term "demonic"

---

25 "When examining demographic trends, the Magisterium of the Church reaffirms
the sacred nature of human life, responsibility for the transmission of life, the inherent
rights of fatherhood and motherhood, [and] the values of marriage and family life, in
the context of which children are the gift of God the Creator. In answer to the supporters of population control and without denying realities, the Church takes the part
of justice by defending the rights of women and men, of families and young people
and those called with the beautiful term *nascituri,* i.e. babies who have been conceived
and are yet to be born and have the right to be born. Noting how population control
can in no way be a substitute for true development, the popes affirm the right of all
people to profit from the abundant resources of the Earth and human intelligence."
Pontifical Council for the Family, *Ethical and Pastoral Dimensions of Population Trends,*
1994, n. 60.

26 The 1994 document from the Pontifical Council for the Family, *Ethical and
Pastoral Dimensions of Population Trends,* gives a solid list of papal pronouncements on
population control from the 60s to the mid-90s: Pope John XXIII, *Mater et Magistra,*
1961; the Second Vatican Council, Pastoral Constitution, *Gaudium et Spes,* 1965; Pope
Paul VI, Address to the U.N. General Assembly, 1965; *Populorum Progressio,* 1967;
Humanae Vitae, 1968; *Octogesima Adveniens,* 1971; Address to the participants of the
world conference of the Food and Agriculture Organization, 1974; Pope John Paul
II, "Message to Christian Families in the Modern World," 1980; *Familiaris Consortio,*
1982; Address to the secretary of the World Population Conference in Mexico City,
1984; Congregation for the Doctrine of the Faith, *Donum Vitae,* 1987; *Sollicitudo
Rei Socialis,* 1987; *Centesimus Annus,* 1991; Address to the Pontifical Academy of
Sciences, 1991; Secretary of State, Cardinal Sodano, address to the U.N. Conference
on Environment and Development in Rio de Janeiro, 1992. See also the Pontifical
Council for the Family's magnificent "Charter on the Rights of the Family."

to describe it, the clear implication of the Church's defensive language is that so much that we hold sacred and sovereign is under attack from Satan and his minions.

The Bible describes at least two systematic programs of population control in its pages: Pharoah's ordering the destruction of Hebrew boys[27] and Herod's attempt to destroy Jesus in the massacre of the Holy Innocents.[28] All the dynamics of modern population control programs are at play in these passages: an evil government threatened by a growing population (or by another King), coercive measures used against vulnerable people, the killing of innocents as a "solution" to the problem, etc. The only real difference between then and now is that in the modern age, females are more targeted for killing than males.[29]

14. How is contraception spiritually evil?

The spiritual evil of contraception has several dimensions to it: the first is its outright rejection of God's command to be generous with life. After God created man and woman, He ordered them to imitate His own generosity in giving life: "Be fertile and multiply!"[30] He said. It is *the sin of disobedience* which closes the human heart to God's express Will for humanity. Instead, the use of contraception loudly proclaims that the human race will be sterile and infertile, with all the consequences that go along with that alien plan.

Secondly, contraception spiritually inverts the *attitude* of being "fertile" and "open to life"[31] and inculcates the attitude of

---

27 Cf. Exodus 1:8-22

28 Cf. Matthew 2:13-18

29 See Question 8 on the issue of "gendercide."

30 Gen 1:28

31 Cf. *Humanae Vitae*, n. 10.

"closedness" to life. This is known as the *contraceptive mentality* which, despite those who naively say that contraception prevents abortion, leads many of its adherents directly to the doors of Planned Parenthood. The second evil of contraception, then, is in the perversion of the mind which is closed to even the possibility of giving life.

The third evil of contraception is its demonic evil of dividing "what God has joined." Every time we see something sacred given to us by God, the devil attempts to infiltrate and divide it. He divided Adam and Eve from each other and divided them as a couple from God and His Plan. We also see him divide flesh and spirit (through sin), man and woman (through homosexuality), parents and children (abortion), husband and wife (divorce), family and society (social breakdown), and finally, the unitive and procreative dimensions of the marital act (as in contraception and *in vitro* fertilization). It is not hard to see how Planned Parenthood serves this divisive agenda either, because their programs constantly divide teens from their parents and their adherents from true faith, etc.

The last dimension mentioned, dividing union and procreation, is where contraception enters most effectively into marriage as a demonic wedge. These two dimensions of the marital act must always remain together, like the two sides of a coin, for the coin to have any value. When we divorce the dimension of *procreation* from the marital act, we have sterile sex that opens the Pandora's box of promiscuity, disease and homosexuality. When we separate the dimension of *union* from the marital act, we begin to "play God" and believe that man has "limitless dominion over his own body,"[32] as evidenced in the hubris of embryonic stem cell research and cloning.

---

32 *Ibid.*, n. 17.

Finally, one of the greatest spiritual evils of contraception is the *deception* that it propagates. Under the guise of some supposed pragmatic good of "preventing unwanted pregnancies," contraception's users are seduced into thinking that they are engaging in something noble which would actually reduce the rate of child-killing. I can't tell you how many intelligent and believing Christians have fallen for this lie! They need to know that *all forms of chemical contraception* partially act as abortifacient drugs by chemically expelling the unborn inhabitants of the womb. Our phrase in English, "swallowing the lie," could not be more evident than in the taking of contraceptive pills.

In sum, contraception is essentially the gateway drug to an immense amount of spiritual evil. It is a bitter pill that has poisoned the human race's very gift of procreation and seduced generations of fertile men and women into sins against God and themselves. The fruit of this spiritual evil is rampant divorce, the widening of the chasm between men and women, rampant promiscuity, pornography, and militant homosexuality. All Christians must reject contraception, and all its works and all its empty promises, in order to truly re-evangelize our society and take it back from the poison of the Evil One.

15. Are abortionists possessed? What about the escorts or the people who work there?

Abortionists and the others who work with them *can* be possessed, but great discernment is needed before any judgment of this sort is made. Sometimes the occult involvement of abortionists, clinic workers or escorts is clear. Anyone who has come into close contact with "escorts" at killing centers knows that some of these people are truly infested with demons. Joe Scheidler of the Pro-Life Action League tells the story of one abortion mill employee who admitted to him that the workers in the clinics were compelled to attack and revile him as a matter of clinic policy. The employee said that many of his companions in the business were Satan worshippers and that they *had* to commit sins to counterbalance the good that was being done by the pro-lifers. That is the perverse "ethic" of Satanists in the abortion business. I might add that I have personally done exorcisms or deliverances on several women whose demonic problems came from their experience of having abortions or confronting the evil practitioners of abortion at close quarters.[33]

Other examples documented in HLI's massive database of abortion violence[34] make the connection between Satanism/witchcraft and abortion clear. For example,

> In 1993, pro-abortion activist Eileen Orstein Janezic murdered 51-year old pro-life activist minister and radio talk show host Jerry Simon. After killing Simon, she held police at bay with a pistol for six hours, while spouting quotes from Anton LaVey's "Satanic Bible." On October 27, 1994, a jury found her guilty of murder and sentenced her to life in prison. During trial, she admitted that she had shot Simon to prove her love of Satan.

Likewise, one former pro-abortion activist admitted:

---

33 I personally conducted a series of exorcisms on a woman, who was part of a pro-life group in the 80s, whose philosophy was to enter abortion clinics intending to stop the killing of babies at least for the day. She remembers entering an abortion mill in Toledo, OH where she was confronted by the sounds and chants of witchcraft rituals being directed against her along with aggressive and cruel treatment at the hands of the abortion clinic employees. The witchcraft "prayers," the acts of violence against her and her delicate emotional state at the time caused her to become possessed. While this is not a common occurrence, the combination of factors was enough to make her a victim of demons and their servants in the abortion industry.

34 See www.prochoiceviolence.com. All of the anecdotes cited in this question are taken from HLI's Abortion Violence database.

I joined the "Freedom of Choice Action League."... Some of them practice witchcraft and sometimes they chalk pentagrams [a Satanic symbol] on the sidewalks. . . . I had written about how they openly practice witchcraft and how the clinic director tells us, every time we beat up the pro-lifers, to cover their cameras. . . . I wrote [in an editorial] that pro-abortionists displayed sex toys in front of children and how they dumped semen and urine on people at national rescues. I personally defaced churches . . . I apologize for that. . . . They hate God, they're anti-Christian . . . Pro-abortionists are the terrorists, not the pro-lifers.[35]

In other cases, the heinous nature of some of the activities of abortion providers gives an insight into the evil that grips them, even though a direct connection with occult or satanic activity may not be evident. For example:

An abortionist in Florida connected to the Wiccan abortionist mentioned above was wont to regularly taunt and deride the pro-lifers who came to pray at his killing center. This abortionist would sometimes come out of the facility with the bloody abortion instruments in his hands after a morning of "business" and shake the *blood* on the pro-lifers.

Joseph Mengele, the famous Nazi mass murderer, known as the "Angel of Death" for his thousands of ghastly medical experiments on living patients in the Auschwitz concentration camp, fled Germany at the end of World War II and became a prominent abortionist in Latin America.

Chicago abortionist, Henry Howard Holmes, labeled "America's Arch Fiend" by the press in the late 1800s, was America's first serial killer, with between fifty and 200 murders committed on people outside the womb. His murders of people inside the womb were exponentially greater in number.

---

35 *The Facts of Life, Inc.* newsletter, December 1992, page 1 and June 1993, pages 4 and 5.

Arizona abortionist Brian Finkel told a reporter, "This is my abortion machine, where I do the Lord's work. I heal the sick with it." "Doctor" Finkel was later convicted of more than 60 counts of sexual abuse and sexual assault and imprisoned for 35 years.

16. If they are not exactly possessed, are they evil?

Many abortionists kill babies not for demonic but rather for *morally sinful* motives like greed, inhumane ideologies or a totally misguided sense of compassion for women. We must be careful about labeling people "possessed," and we must pray fervently for these people. There is every indication that abortionists are truly desperate people who need prayer more than anything. Mark Crutcher's groundbreaking book, *Lime Five*,[36] has exposed the completely degenerate lifestyles of many people who practice abortion. If abortionists have any dialogue with their consciences at all, they will often confess that they know that they should give up the practice of abortion, but when they try, the Accuser's voice intervenes: "You have a lot of blood on your hands, you can't leave now;" or "There's no hope for someone who has killed so many babies;" etc. The devil does not allow his servitors to have easy conversions without a fight, and this is why they need the prayers of all Christians to bring them out of their slavery to the darkness.

In 2003, I met a woman who ran a Marie Stopes clinic that did clandestine abortions in a rural area in Kenya. She sounded very much like an American feminist when rattling off her pre-packaged epithets about "reproductive choice," but after some probing I found out that she was a Catholic who had been trained in Nairobi's Kenyatta Hospital by British doctors and

---

36 Mark Crutcher, *Lime Five: Exploited by Choice*, Life Dynamics, Inc.: Denton, TX, 1996.

nurses. Although she needed and opted for the high-paying job at this clinic, her conscience kept bothering her. She felt trapped in serving this evil agenda, until some local priests kindly offered to help find her another job. It was not clear to me whether she would ultimately decide in favor of her conscience and leave the Marie Stopes clinic. The money of the abortion industry is seductive, and deciding against it is a tough decision for those who live in impoverished societies.

Even if people in the abortion industry have given themselves over to a life of sin or occult practices, we must never give up hope for their salvation. We must constantly pray for their conversions and trust that the Lord will use our witness to them for their salvation in His own time and way. The conversion of Dr. Bernard Nathanson, a key player in the legalization of abortion in the late 1960s and 70s, provides abundant evidence that prayer can work miracles, even for those totally immersed in evil.

Likewise, Norma McCorvey and Sandra Cano were *used* by the abortion industry to bring the 1973 court cases that eventually legalized abortion (McCorvey in *Roe v. Wade*) and obliterated any limits to its practice (Cano in *Doe v. Bolton*) respectively. Norma McCorvey tells the touching story of a nine-year-old girl named Emily reaching out to her in Christian love as the main force leading her out of the abortion business. Her autobiography is called, appropriately, *Won by Love*.[37] Ms. McCorvey eventually even converted to Catholicism. In Christ, every soul has hope for salvation, for as St. Paul says, "Despite the increase of sin, grace has far surpassed it."[38]

---

37 Norma McCorvey, *Won by Love*, Thomas Nelson Publishers: Nashville, TN, 1997.

38 Rom 5:20

17. How has this evil spilled over into American society?

There are innumerable ways in which the abortion mindset affects American society, not the least of which is seen in the corruption of youth culture. I am not attempting here to analyze the complexities of American youth culture; I am just offering some simple observations and examples of the devastating effect that the killing of one-third of all children in the United States since 1973 has had on many members of the two generations that have grown up under the terror of the abortion regime.

The first and most devastating effect of the abortion culture is the "normalizing" effect of murder. John Kippley, founder of the Couple to Couple League, wrote a provocative pamphlet called, *From Contraception to Abortion...to Columbine*,[39] in which he traces the history of interlinked mindsets which, in his estimation, led to the culture in which we have seen so many mass killings in recent years. He cites first the rejection of the traditional Christian position on contraception by the Protestant churches, beginning in 1930, and then the mirror of that in the widespread Catholic dissent to the papal encyclical on birth control, *Humanae Vitae,* in the late 60s. The same era saw the massive promotion of the birth control Pill and the capitulation of the medical profession to the idea that babies could be chemically killed with impunity. There followed the Supreme Court decisions, *Griswold v. Connecticut* (legalizing birth control for married couples in 1965), *Eisenstadt v. Baird* (legalizing birth control for singles in 1972), and *Roe v. Wade* (legalizing abortion in 1973), all based on the flawed logic of the "right to privacy." From these, Kippley said, society's attitude toward killing very easily changed. The "radical subjectivism of freedom from any external constraints" enshrined by the Court made the kill-

---

39 John F. Kippley, *From Contraception to Abortion...to Columbine*, Couple to Couple League, Cincinnati, OH, n.d.

ing of innocents a simple matter of privacy and personal choice. Columbine was its logical conclusion.

Secondly, it appears that for most people under the age of 35, "choice" has become an absolute value in itself and something to celebrate in art and culture. The crassest of all expressions of this was clearly the art display created by Yale University student, Aliza Schvarts, in 2008. Ms. Schvarts claims to have privately inseminated herself with donor sperm numerous times over a nine month period, achieving at least two pregnancies which she claims to have aborted on her own using the RU-486 pill. Ms. Schvarts then used her own blood and the blood from the aborted babies to create an art display wherein the blood was mixed with Vaseline and pasted between two sheets of plastic wrapped around a cube that hung from the ceiling. She also used the blood to paint the backdrop of the display. This sad and disgusting display was Schvarts' senior art project and it was initially defended by Yale University under the auspices of "freedom of expression." To this day, Schvarts defends her actions and "artwork" as a perfectly legitimate assertion of her rights in American society.

Finally, abortion has contributed mightily to the fracturing of American society into essentially two opposed value camps: pagan and Christian; or those who see all truth as relative and those who acknowledge that objective right and wrong really exist and have a claim on us. These differences are reflected roughly in our political divisions, in our social permissiveness versus true moral values, in the various opposing cultural movements which are growing in intensity each day, in the corrupt media versus the new alternative media, etc. All these divisions reflect diametrically differing views over whether abortion should be legal or not. More examples could be cited of the negative effect of the abortion mentality on Americans and our culture, but suffice it to say that the radical deformation of basic human values is the most overwhelming and long-term effect of this evil.

18. Can a whole society be possessed?

Just as a person can be possessed, it is possible for a society to be possessed in an analogous way. Demonic possession is of the body, not of the soul, *per se*, so we can speak of possession of the "body politic" of a society in an analogous way. The members and organs of the body (politic) can be under the domination of the possessing demon and he can commandeer or overpower the spiritual faculties of the soul (mind and will) in the infested/possessed state. In societies as in persons, there always remains that basic human endowment of inner freedom, which assures that the person or society is never without its capacity to choose the right path.

Fr. José Antonio Fortea, the famous Spanish exorcist, applies the analogy of possession to a society. He recalls reading the Books of the Maccabees in an entirely new light when he realized that the Maccabees were trying to accomplish an expulsion of a demonic possession that had taken over the land of Israel.[40] The story describes every level of demonic activity from temptation to oppression to infestation to possession. In just the first chapter of 1 Maccabees, each of these stages is described in some detail, beginning with the name and description of the possessing force; namely, Antiochus Epiphanes, who is called a "sinful offshoot" (1 Mc 1:10) and who invaded and ravaged Palestine after the death of Alexander the Great. The following passages describe the advance of evil into a full-blown possession of a society:

---

40 Father Fortea explained his idea of the possession of a whole society at a conference on healing and deliverance at Mundelein Seminary near Chicago in August of 2007.

Temptation: "In those days there appeared in Israel men who were breakers of the law, and they seduced many people, saying, 'Let us go and make an alliance with the Gentiles all around us; since we separated from them many evils have come upon us'"(v. 11). "He spoke to them deceitfully in peaceful terms and won their trust" (v. 30a). "Then the king wrote to his whole kingdom that all should be one, each abandoning his particular customs. All the Gentiles conformed to the command of the king, and many Israelites were in favor of his religion" (vv. 41-43).

Oppression: "Then he attacked the city suddenly, in a great onslaught, and destroyed many of the people in Israel. He plundered the city and set fire to it, demolished its houses and surrounding walls, took captive women and children and seized the cattle" (v. 30b).

Infestation: "There they installed a sinful race, perverse men, who fortified themselves inside it, storing up weapons and provisions, and depositing there the plunder they had collected from Jerusalem" (vv. 34-35).

Possession: "He insolently invaded the sanctuary and took away the golden altar, the lampstand for the light with all its fixtures…and the golden ornament on the façade of the temple. He stripped off everything…[and] went back to his own country after he had spoken with great arrogance and shed much blood" (vv. 21-24). "The citadel became an ambush against the sanctuary, and a wicked adversary to Israel at all times. And they shed innocent blood around the sanctuary; they defiled the sanctuary.…Her sanctuary was as desolate as a wilderness" (vv. 36-37.39).

Demonic control: "Then the king sent messengers…ordering them to follow customs foreign to their land; to prohibit holocausts, sacrifices and libations in the sanctuary, to profane the sabbaths…to desecrate the sanctuary…to build pagan altars…to sacrifice swine…to leave their sons uncircumcised, and to let themselves be defiled with every kind of impurity and abomination….Whoever refused to act according to the command of the king should be put to death" (vv. 44-50).

These brief quotes show clearly how the possession of a society happens. It always proceeds in stages and ends up in bondage of the person—or society. The Maccabean Revolt described in both books further highlights, however, that no possessed person ever loses his freedom completely, nor does any society. There is always an element of human freedom that can never be suppressed. In fact, God can even use the state of possession to bring a person or a society to a new awareness of self and maturity. In this case, the Jewish feast of Hanukah was instituted in the life and history of the people of Israel as a remembrance of the re-dedication of the sanctuary (Temple) once the evil force had been expelled. This shows how God can bring much good out of evil.

19. Is American society possessed or becoming possessed?

In a very real way, the demon of child sacrifice "entered" American society on January 22, 1973 through the doorways of the Supreme Court decisions *Roe v. Wade* and *Doe v. Bolton*, which allowed abortion "on demand" for literally any reason during all nine months of pregnancy. That decision of the highest faculty of "judgment" in our body politic gave permission for the process of possession to begin. Prior to that, America was being *tempted* by Planned Parenthood's pro-abortion propaganda for many decades; there were also numerous cases of *oppression* (attacks) at the state level where abortion activists tried to force their killing practices on the rest of society, but the *infestation* came when the Supreme Court decisions flung open the door to Moloch and gave him permission to go on his killing spree throughout our great land. I do not believe that full possession by the abortion demon has yet taken place in American society, due to the restraining force that we call the pro-life movement and the restraining force of God's grace that Paul refers to in 2 Thes 2:1-12.[41] However, the power of the demon over our institutions and society is clearly far advanced.

The analogy of the city whose walls have been breached applies here; once the demon gains entrance to the city (i.e. the person), the body becomes infested and the demon begins to assert more control over the body and faculties. The analogy to a society is similar. America's "mind" is embodied by the organs that do its thinking; in this case, the educational system and the public information system (media). These are totally captivated by abortion. America's "will" consists in the decision-making organs of the body politic, namely, the executive, legislative and judicial branches of government, institutions which have shown themselves to be almost totally devoid of righteousness in abortion politics. America's "imagination" consists in those institutions that convey "images" to the public, namely, the entertainment and music industries. These are universally pro-abortion in their leanings and products.

---

41 The famous Catholic preacher, Fr. John Corapi, has often commented on this passage and refers to the Holy Eucharist as the spiritual force that "restrains" (2 Thes 2:6) the "man of lawlessness" (2 Thes 2:3) who is so powerful a force of destruction in modern society.

Figure 7: Diabolical possession of persons and societies

Persons	Demonic Action	Society
Mind: intellectual faculty	Demon overpowers the mind with lies and deceptions	Educational and informational organs of public discourse
Emotions and passions: imaginative faculty	Demon penetrates and afflicts the most vulnerable part of the human soul	Image-makers of society: music and entertainment industries
Will: volitional faculty	Demon coerces the will and forces acquiescence	Political faculties: Exccutive, Legislative and Judicial powers
Body	Demon possesses and controls the body	The people (i.e., the "body politic")
Personal faith as a necessary condition for liberation: exorcism as the spiritual force to drive out a demon	Demon resists and attacks any spiritual force that seeks to free the victim	The Church of Christ as a necessary condition for liberation of a society: Church authority as the spiritual force to drive out demons

In a diabolical possession, demons don't need full understanding or agreement to do their evil once they have entered; they just need *acquiescence* of will. The same happens in a populace where a demon can gain increasing control of the culture and its institutions over time with the acquiescence of the people. In modern American society, just a minority of abortion-obsessed individuals controls the passive majority who support the demonic activity by acquiescence, if not by full agreement. There is no such thing as "neutrality" on the abortion issue. An apathetic society on the issue of abortion is a *compliant* society to the demonic will.

A possessed individual can only obtain his freedom from demonic forces by turning to *a superior spiritual force* that will help him be free. "Setting the captives free"[42] is one of the proper roles of religion, and the more the individual turns his soul to Christ through the Church, the more hope he has of being liberated from his demons. Making religious acts of mind and will asserts, however weakly, his inner freedom and identity over against the possessing power.

A society, in the same way, cannot be free of its demons without the help of a religious authority that is stronger than the demons. The devil does not fear human ingenuity or politics. He controls and manipulates these. Nor does he fear prophets. These he kills. What he fears is an overwhelming religious authority endowed with a divine commission to vanquish his kingdom, and that is the Church that Christ founded.

The pro-life movement represents that relatively weak but distinct force of religious conscience *from within* a society. Pro-lifers are members of the body politic itself, and by their voices and activities they *assert* society's ultimate freedom from demonic control. As a grassroots, de-centralized lay movement, however, pro-lifers as such will never be strong enough, resourceful enough or powerful enough to *liberate* a society from demonic infestation. The pro-life movement is not a strong enough spiritual authority in and of itself. An infested society needs a *Church Militant* to free it from infestation. The Church's divinely-ap-

---

42 Cf. Is 42:7

pointed mission is to *bind* society's demons and command them to *loosen* their grip on the body politic.[43]

It is therefore no surprise that the culture of death has grown in direct proportion to the weakening of the Catholic Church and her leadership in the past forty years. When the Church is weak in carrying out its God-given mission, all of society is weak. When God is driven out or unwelcome in a culture, demons enter in. Only the re-establishment of a strong, authoritative Church will heal and liberate the world from abortion. The demon of child sacrifice, once invited and entered, will not leave voluntarily. It must be driven out by the Church.

20. What is spiritual warfare?

Spiritual warfare is both a recognition that the Church's mission is to battle the kingdom of darkness on this earth and an engagement in such a battle. The weapons of spiritual warfare are just that, spiritual: prayer, conscientious objection and the authoritative expulsion of evil spirits from people and places. Spiritual warfare is entirely peaceful in a civic, social and political sense. The only ones who are negatively affected by spiritual warfare are evil spirits.

21. Is spiritual warfare in the pro-life cause violent?

As mentioned above, spiritual warfare is not a material form of warfare. As such, there is never any justification or excuse for violence of any sort, and anyone who would use the Church or the tenets of spiritual warfare to justify violence is simply making an illegitimate argument for change that the Church neither makes nor accepts. While the Church does have a well-established teaching concerning the principles for legitimate self-defense

---

43 Cf. Mt 16:19

and "just war," that teaching concerns material warfare between nations and has nothing to do with spiritual warfare.

22. What forms of spiritual warfare are appropriate in pro-life work?

Prayer is the primary weapon of spiritual warfare when understood as an act of the whole Church. Lay persons pray powerfully when they stand in front of abortion centers and plead for the lives of the unborn, but they need the leadership of clergy to guide them in the formal public prayers of the Church at these clinics, which could include even deliverance prayers, or exorcism prayers if properly authorized.

Other types of spiritual warfare are the various means of *witness and conscientious objection* that have a public character. In Nicaragua in 2006, for example, the retired cardinal and the new archbishop led a pro-life march of *200,000 people* through the streets of Managua, prior to a vote to remove abortion from the country's criminal code. Faced with this tremendous act of conscientious objection, the politicians voted 59-0 to eliminate abortion entirely! This manifestation of the popular will was totally peaceful, but it was also motivated by and presided over by bishops. Other forms of spiritual warfare can be boycotts, public relations campaigns, organized protests, etc.

23. What forms of spiritual warfare can the lay faithful carry out at abortion mills or anywhere else?

Two forms of spiritual warfare are most appropriate at abortion mills: *organized prayer and sidewalk counseling*. I emphasize "organized prayer" because, too often, the people who gather at abortion mills do so with very little internal discipline, and their meetings devolve into loose talkative groups rather than disciplined spiritual warfare. The areas in front of and around abortion mills are always hotbeds of demonic activity, so it is necessary that the people who do this ministry maintain a strong sense of discipline, organization and prayer.

I strongly advocate the praying of the St. Michael the Archangel prayer by the laity at these places of death. There is no prohibition to praying the Exorcism of Pope Leo XIII privately by any priest who goes to a mill, as long as it is done discreetly and with no fanfare that would give the impression that the priest is performing a solemn exorcism. Spontaneous prayers of deliverance and binding always effectively confront the spiritual stronghold at an abortion mill, and they are entirely non-violent. One must always guard against a superstitious mindset toward deliverance, however. Such prayers are not a form of "Catholic magic" that shuts down clinics. They are exercises of spiritual authority and faith, which always have some spiritual effect on the demonic forces that are gathered at that physical location, even if the effects are not immediately seen or known.

Sidewalk counseling is also a form of spiritual warfare when it is done prayerfully and professionally. There are some simple techniques that one can learn in order to be an effective sidewalk counselor and various groups that offer such training. Whenever there are sidewalk counselors doing their work, it is also recommended that there be a team of prayer warriors to do nothing but pray and support them in this work.

One other form of spiritual warfare that needs much more discussion and commitment on the part of the Church is the *establishment of Eucharistic adoration chapels* in parishes near abortion mills. The intent of an established chapel near an abortion mill would be to bind the power of abortion's evil and bring souls to conversion. The growth of perpetual adoration chapels in parishes across America, I believe, has already been very effective in reducing both the number of abortionists and death clinics in America. More than anything, the establishment of a perpetual adoration chapel near an abortion mill signifies that a local church community is serious about ending abortion in their neighborhood. Every publicly-known abortionist's name should be enshrined before a monstrance in a perpetual adoration chapel near the place where his or her dirty business is conducted.

24. How can pro-lifers on the front lines protect themselves spiritually?

Those who do hand-to-hand combat with the devil at abortion mills or who have direct contact with rabid abortion proponents must spiritually protect themselves and their families from the power of evil. While we have weapons of righteousness for the "destruction of [spiritual] strongholds,"[44] the devil also has his own weapons of darkness for the destruction of the life of grace, and he uses them against those who oppose his kingdom.

The most basic form of spiritual protection is simply living in a state of grace, defined as keeping one's soul free of mortal sin and striving to overcome all venial sin in one's life. An added spiritual protection comes from actively developing the theological, cardinal and moral virtues in one's life and trying to discern God's Will on a daily basis. Living a fervent life of grace should normally be sufficient for spiritual protection, even on the front lines of combat with the devil and his minions.

A method that all soldiers can use to assure protection from demonic powers is the practice of binding evil spirits. Fundamentally, a "binding" prayer is simply a spontaneous prayer that is said when one discerns the presence of some evil force acting in his life or in the physical location that he is in. A

---

44 2 Cor 10:4

binding prayer simply restricts the ability of an unclean spirit to harm, seduce or manipulate human beings. Any binding prayer consists of three elements: the Name of Jesus, the name of the unclean spirit and a command to be bound.

At an abortion mill, for example, a person can bind any of the unclean spirits that are present at that spiritual stronghold: the spirits of abortion, birth control, coercion, fear, greed, violence, witchcraft, etc. "In the Name of Jesus, I bind the spirit of _____." A prayer of this type often has to be repeated for effect, and the results of it are not always evident to our eyes; but the demons understand the nature of a binding prayer because it always restricts the scope of their violence in some way. A binding prayer is more effective when two or three gather in the Name of Jesus to pray, and it is always an expression of the authority over demons that all Christians have been given by our Lord (cf. Mk 16:17).

25. What is the spiritual significance of pregnancy care centers?

Pregnancy care centers are the humble workers of the pro-life movement whose tangible services back up the spiritual authority of the Church with the corporal works of mercy. The Church does not ignore the temporal reality of the people who are caught in the vice grip of the culture of death but "loves them both," as Dr. John Willke has said.

These centers often save babies *by facilitating the change of an abortion-minded (or abortion-vulnerable) woman's "choice."* This in itself is a spiritual act since the power to make decisions is rooted in the will, one of the spiritual faculties of the soul. Just as a possessed person cannot be liberated without some act of cooperation with God's grace, so the woman must say "no" to the demon of abortion that tempts her. The pregnancy care center workers cannot make the decision for her. She must be willing to reject the temptation to do such an evil act.

For this reason, pregnancy care center workers perform *spiritual works of mercy* by exposing the temptations to murder, by "instructing the ignorant," by "counseling the doubtful" about the sanctity of human life and by praying for those who need it most. We ought to be extremely grateful for the millions of babies whose lives have been saved through the self-sacrificing commitment of those who work in pregnancy care centers. We will never know how many millions of women, men and babies have been helped with the tangible charity of these champions of the Church.

26. What is the most successful model of pro-life spiritual warfare?

The most successful model of pro-life spiritual warfare is the "Jericho" model. The passage about the siege of Jericho[45] gives the template that is most effective for the Church Militant's battle against the culture of death. It starts with Joshua's vision of St. Michael the Archangel[46] and the promise that God has already delivered Jericho and its king into Joshua's power.[47] Spiritual warfare is always based upon the fundamental conviction that God has *already* won the battle and sent us in to fight it with full assurance of victory.

All parts of this model make up the Church Militant marching into battle: heaven, the hierarchical Church leadership, the clergy, the talents of professionals and the combined prayers of the people of God. When the full force of the obedient and disciplined

---

45   Josh 5:13-6:20

46   Cf. 5:14. The mysteroius heavenly figure that confronts Joshua here calls himself, "the captain of the host of the Lord."

47   Cf. 6:1

Church is brought to the "gates of hell" of the abortion industry, there is no force of demons that can withstand the spiritual onslaught. Everyone knows how this story ends: the walls of Jericho came crumbling down without so much as a single shot being fired.

This passage is often used by opponents of the pro-life movement to accuse us of advocating violence, which is explicitly forbidden by our Christian code of ethics except in legitimate self-defense. The truth is that our Christian "power" is not human; it is one of blessing and love, which has nothing to do with violence and seeks only the conversion of the perpetrators of the real violence of abortion. In effect, the Church doesn't need to commit any violent acts; we have *a more powerful weapon*, prayer.

Figure 8: Joshua and the Church Militant

The People of Israel battle Jericho	The Church of Christ battles abortion
Joshua meets "the Captain of the host of the Lord" (Josh 5:14)	St. Michael and the heavenly host are involved in our battle
"The Lord" announces that Jericho has already been delivered into his hands (Josh 6:2)	The firm post-Resurrection conviction of the Christian Church that the battle is already won, just not yet engaged
Joshua worships and leads (Josh 5:14-15; 6:2.6)	The local bishop
Picked troops (Josh 6:3.9)	Professionals and those faithful on the "frontlines" of the culture war
Priests blowing horns (Josh 6:4.13)	Priests preaching, speaking and teaching—to both the faithful and society at large

Priests carrying the "Holy of Holies" (Josh 6:4.6)	Priests and religious carrying the spiritual resources of our Church into battle
The "Holy of Holies"	The Body, Blood, Soul and Divinity of Jesus Christ in the Eucharist
The "Ark of the Lord" (Josh 6:4-13)	The Virgin Mary
People of Israel in battle formation (Josh 6:7)	The Church following its strong pastoral leadership
Walking in silence around the city for six days (Josh 6:14)	Patience in confronting and uprooting the abortion demon deeply embedded in society
Walking seven times around the city on the seventh day only (Josh 6:16)	Obedience to God's command and marshalling the full spiritual force of the Church
The people all shout in unison at the signal of Joshua (Josh 6:10.20a)	The powerful force of the collective voice of all levels of the Church speaking and acting in unison
"The wall collapsed..." (Josh 6:20c)	"The gates of hell shall not prevail against it" (Mt 16:18). (Cf. Douay-Rheims version of Mt. 16:18.)
"... and they stormed the city in a frontal attack and took it" (Josh 6:20d).	The Christian faith re-claims the previously possessed "territory" of the abortion industry and mentality

27. What are the two most effective forces in the American pro-life movement today?

Along these lines, I consider the two most effective groups in the pro-life movement to be Msgr. Philip Reilly's "Helpers of God's Precious Infants" and the relatively new "40 Days for Life" movement. The "Helpers" are explicitly dedicated to implementing the Jericho model, bringing the power of Christ to the gates of the abortion hell. Monsignor Reilly is a long-time pro-life activist, a faithful priest and former seminary rector from Brooklyn, and from his many years of experience, he developed a simple form of combating the abortion demon based upon the many trials and errors of the pro-life movement up to that point. He created the system of prayer vigils and processions that go out to the places of killing.

His refreshingly spiritual approach to the abortion holocaust mobilizes tens of thousands of people all around the world every year to participate in spiritual "prayer vigils." These consist of Masses in churches near abortion mills, followed by Eucharistic Adoration. The attendees march in procession to a nearby abortion mill, praying the Rosary, while some remain behind, praying in front of the Blessed Sacrament. At the mill, they intercede in silence for the staff of the abortion centers, the clientele, and any others who support the business. Monsignor asks people to spiritually "go to Calvary" and stay there interceding for the innocent ones being crucified by abortion, as well as their executioners. The "Helpers" also train sidewalk counselors for the ministry of personally inviting people out of the darkness and into the Light of Christ.

The "Helpers" movement has formed and mobilized the Church Militant more than any other organization I have seen, and they work closely with Human Life International around the world. Their prayer vigils have successfully closed clinics, converted abortionists, caused women and men to choose life, given the people of God effective leadership and, perhaps the greatest miracle of all, they have gotten over 100 bishops to go to abortion mills to pray!

The "40 Days for Life" movement began in 2004 in College Station, TX under the leadership of David Bereit and Shawn Carney and employed a similar idea as the "Helpers" in fighting the spiritual force of abortion. They use the biblical notion of Christ's own 40 days of prayer and fasting in the desert and confrontation with Satan before His public ministry as a model of the spiritual warfare against our modern demons. The fruitfulness of an apostolic work is its own testimony. Mr. Bereit claims that the "40 Days for Life" movement now spans 282 cities across all 50 of the United States, six Canadian provinces, plus locations in Australia, Northern Ireland and Denmark. The movement has brought perhaps tens of thousands of people into the spiritual battle against the culture of death and saved more than 2168 babies at the time of this writing, according to their best estimates. May the Lord continue to bless their work!

28. What role does the Church have to play in fighting the culture of death?

As hinted at in the last question, the Church is the only religious authority that has the spiritual power to free a society of its abortion demons. "The Church" means the Church that Christ founded, which subsists in the Catholic Church and which is a communion of believing persons uniting heaven and earth. This "Church Militant," led by consecrated churchmen with spiritual authority, buoyed by the holy power of its religious orders, fully employing the dynamic gifts and prayers of the laity, is the Church that brings the power of Christ to the gates of Jericho.

This warfare is not the responsibility of the clergy alone or the laity alone but of all its members together. The angels and saints of heaven are also involved, as they assist the Church Militant in its earthly battles against the forces of evil.

Furthermore, the Church Militant is perfectly equipped to battle the demon of abortion and the whole culture of death. The Church confronts the false "gospel" of radical feminist rhetoric with the Truth of Jesus Christ in its well-elaborated *social doctrine and moral teachings*. The *Catechism*, the intellectual patrimony of the Church, and the Church's universities and seminaries[48] are strong weapons against the lies and deceptions of the devil. Furthermore, the Catholic Church has such an impressive system of parishes, schools and healthcare facilities that its actual ability to deliver the message to youths and adults is potentially greater than any single private institution on the face of the earth.

To combat the appalling rhetoric of "abortion as sacrament,"[49] the Catholic Church has immense *spiritual and sacramental resources* that it can bring to the warfare. Eucharistic and Marian devotions are the most potent weapons against these evils, as well as devotion to the angels, especially St. Michael the Archangel. No abortion demon could possibly withstand the sacramental authority of the Church *if it were invoked properly*.

Finally, with its *hierarchical authority*, the Church could potentially tear down every spiritual stronghold of evil in our world. It is for this reason that the Church has been entrusted the power of the keys "to bind and to loose"[50] and to stand before the gates of hell to batter them with the authority of Christ. We

---

48 That is, those universities and seminaries that are orthodox in doctrine and practice.

49 See Appendix A.

50 Mt 16:19

have His promise that they "will not prevail" against that authority when it is properly applied.[51] Priests and bishops have the authority to name these demons, confront them and cast them out as exorcists do. Such a confrontation requires immense moral courage both on the part of our ecclesiastical leaders who wield it and on the part of the people who must support and cooperate with that authority when it is exercised.

29. How can I get my priest to speak more from the pulpit about abortion and contraception?

I get asked this question on every continent and in every place I speak, and my answer is always the same. If a priest is not actively preaching about the life issues, which are of the very core of the Church's prophetic witness in the modern era, then we must ask him to do so. Some need only a stimulus from the laity, and they will respond. If the invitation is made and still there is no response, then other initiatives of the laity are possible: they can invite the priest to an abortion clinic to experience the abortion business firsthand; they can provide good pro-life homily notes to the priest; or just tell him how desperately his leadership is needed in this area, and see if he responds.

It's worth trying to help a priest to be faithful to his own vocation, but it is also important not to waste too much time on faithless or cowardly priests. They will receive their own judgment before the Throne of God,[52] and it will be severe. While the least of Christ's brethren are suffering cruel deaths in abortion chambers down the street from many churches, the gutless shepherds will have to account for their silence.

---

51 Mt 16:18

52 Cf. Mt. 25: 31

I always discourage complaining too much about weak or negligent priests and recommend much more focus on the future. It is much more productive for the laity to assist the younger generation of priests and seminarians in integrating the pro-life priority into their priesthood. We must also strongly support those few clergy who actually do speak out on the life issues, because they will be attacked—most ferociously from *within* the Church! Christ the Good Shepherd will take care of the rest.

30. Why do we need priestly and episcopal leadership in the pro-life movement?

The bishops are the general officers of the Church Militant in this confrontation with evil. They are the strategic minds and the executive authority that presides over the Church that Christ established as a hierarchical institution. The bishops are the leaders of this holy militia. They have been entrusted with the divine authority to teach, to sanctify and to govern the Church for the salvation of souls.

"Whoever wants to be a bishop aspires to a noble task,"[53] says St. Paul to Timothy; yet, he who accepts election to the office of bishop in today's Church must do so with fear and trembling because of the severity of the judgment he will undergo by the Chief Shepherd if he does not use this authority for the actual mission of extending Christ's kingdom over against the reign of Satan. This includes using the episcopal authority to end the vicious slaughter of the innocents, whom many papal pronouncements in recent times have told us are the poorest of the poor and "the least brethren" of Christ. The defense of the flock and the use of the Church's spiritual resources in that defense is the greatest pastoral need of our day. "When much has been given a

---

53   1 Tm 3:1

man, much will be required of him."[54] Bishops have been given the greatest share in the Priesthood of Jesus Christ and will be held accountable for their proper use of the spiritual power that has been entrusted to them.

The same can be said for Catholic priests who have been entrusted with the care of souls. Within their legitimate sphere of authority, they have the strictest obligation to both uphold the teaching of the Church in all matters and to form the Church Militant for battle. Clerical dissent or even silence about matters related to faith and morals constitute inexcusable spiritual negligence in the face of such seductive propaganda campaigns of the culture of death that entice and seduce the sheep of their flocks to sin. The judgment on clerics who live lavish lifestyles, lead the flock astray through preaching false doctrines or are silent while their innocent parishioners are being murdered will be stringent.

31. Will bringing the Eucharist to an abortion clinic shut it down?

Retired Bishop James Sullivan of the Diocese of Fargo, ND did this in the 90s, but it is not a common practice at all. He conducted a number of Helpers-style prayer processions to the Fargo Women's Health Organization in the late 1990s, *carrying the Blessed Sacrament himself,* accompanied by many of his priests vested in liturgical garb and followed by more than a thousand people each time. The killing center was just sixteen blocks down the street from St. Mary's Cathedral and was one of only two in the whole State of North Dakota.

It is interesting to note that the Fargo Women's Health Organization, which had been operative since 1981, shut its doors in 2001, claiming its closure was a "business decision." They were

---

54 Lk 12:48

unable to find abortionists to do their dirty work. In the meantime, Planned Parenthood consolidated a number of smaller, failing abortion businesses, and now there is only one abortion mill in the whole state of North Dakota. Did the Eucharistic processions have an effect on the closure of the abortion mill? The connection between the two seems more than a coincidence, even if the abortion *business* may have changed venues.

Some say that we should not bring the Eucharist to the abortion mills for fear of desecration or trivialization, and I agree that extreme caution is always needed for any act involving the Eucharist. It may even be erroneously interpreted as a kind of Eucharistic "magic" which brings an automatic result, and we must guard against this kind of superstition.

Notwithstanding the need for a maximum degree of prudence in bringing the "Holy of Holies" into the abortion battle, Bishop Sullivan's example is instructive; namely, that the Jericho Church went out to the "gates of hell" in a significant way and the result was powerful against the evil of abortion. The four-star general of the Church Militant in that diocese carried Christ Himself to the place of death, with his priests in attendance dressed in battle garb. The picked troops of the pro-life movement prepared the event carefully, even getting a police escort for the mighty procession. The people of God came out in huge numbers to peacefully pray for an end to the killing, and the walls of that place of death came tumbling down in time. This is not hard to understand from a spiritual warfare point of view. When the Church Militant gets active, "the gates of hell" cannot prevail,[55] pure and simple.

---

55 Mt 16:18 (Douay-Rheims version)

32. Can a priest do an exorcism over a functioning abortion mill?

Yes, priests can pray the Exorcism of Pope Leo XIII privately at abortion mills, but they can only do so *publicly* with the authorization of the local bishop. That is clear from the 1985 statement of the Congregation of the Doctrine of the Faith.[56] There is one US diocese I know of that has authorized several priests to officially conduct prayers of exorcism at a local abortion mill, and so far, the fruit of the prayer seems to be an increased effectiveness in sidewalk counseling in saving babies and changing minds and hearts.[57] In training the priests, I emphasized that the Church's exorcism prayer is not a Catholic magic wand to shut down abortion mills. It is simply the authority of the Church to restrict and expel demons from that place. In doing so, hearts and minds are changed.

Having spent many years on the front lines of the abortion battle, I have prayed private prayers of deliverance at abortion mills in many places with incredible effect. In one very dramatic case at a Florida abortion mill, an angry client was aggressively taking pictures of the pro-lifers with her cell phone to harass them. However, when I spoke to her she told me directly that she had two children already and could not afford another child. I prayed deliverance prayers for her, and fifteen minutes later, she left the killing center, never to return. Her unexplained transformation from an aggressive, angry woman to a compassionate mother was, undoubtedly, the result of that prayer.

---

56 Letter of the Congregation of the Doctrine of the Faith (*Inde Ab Aliquot Annis*), *On the Current Norms Governing Exorcism*, September 29, 1985.

57 In fact, a recent report at www.prolifecorner.com (May 29, 2010) indicates that the business at said abortion mill has been "cut at least in half" since the priests have been praying there.

33. What should be done to spiritually cleanse a former killing center?

There have been many instances of abortion mills going out of business and pro-life people buying them or taking them over for pro-life purposes. It is extremely important to spiritually cleanse a place where abortions were committed before that place is used again for any reason. In most cases, a simple blessing over the place with the sprinkling of holy water will go a long way to cleanse the space of demonic influences that may linger there. However, given the nature of the demonic killing that took place in those premises, a solemn exorcism should be performed at the place to assure that its evil is *driven* out. Again, the use of the Exorcism of Pope Leo XIII will require the permission of the local bishop, since this type of blessing can be seen as a formal act. Otherwise, any blessing by a priest will normally be sufficient to expel the evil presences from that place no longer given over to the service of the devil.

34. Should pro-lifers "buy out" abortion centers or pay off the abortionists to get them out of the business?

Great discernment is needed in situations where pro-lifers have a chance to buy out an abortion business. On the one hand it may be the best way to stop the killing by literally taking over the killing center itself. Some abortionists stay in the business only because they have money problems or fear a very real economic loss to them if they leave, so an offer to buy them out can free them up to leave the dirty business definitively. The economic resources of the Christian community should always be put at the service of babies, and wealthy Christians have an obligation to look for these opportunities. If there is a *well-founded* hope of getting an abortionist to quit by buying him out, then let the

Church pay him off and ransom the children from his suction machine.

When St. John Vianney wanted to break the little southern French town of Ars of its sinful habit of secular dances, he would regularly find the fiddler, pay him his fee and send him away without him having to earn his money on something immoral! In this way, together with his intransigent preaching against immorality, he was successful in curbing an immoral practice in a short time. He attacked both the supply and the demand for the evil thing.

A greater discernment is needed on buying out abortion clinics, however, because those who kill also lie. If pro-lifers are not certain beyond a reasonable doubt that the abortionist will close his doors and go away, then buying him out could be a well-meaning but very expensive mistake and not save any babies. An abortionist may just re-invest his money into another center and shift the killing to another venue or go to another town and open up shop. We must be "clever as serpents and innocent as doves" in these matters and pray for God's guidance to know what may be the best course of action.

35. Do women who have abortions get possessed?

It is *possible* for women to become infested with a demon by the act of abortion, but as far as I can tell this is not common. In order for a demon to enter through an abortion, it would have to be either by a deliberate act of a Satanist or witch directly targeting the woman while the abortion is going on, or by a demon entering simply through the trauma of the abortion itself. The latter is more likely, given the general demonic character of the industry, but it would be impossible to know the number of women who are so affected by abortion.

I have, however, personally done deliverance prayers on women whose demons entered through the act of abortion. Also, in the post-abortion healing ministry, we have seen women literally "exorcised" by the healing prayer that frees them from their spiritual desolation. Abortion is a traumatic experience, physically, emotionally and spiritually, and demons can enter through this trauma. Much of the post-abortion suffering is spiritual as well as emotional.

This does not mean that all women who have abortions become infested by demons. God's protective grace and guardian angels operate in mysterious ways to protect people even in situations of grave mortal sin. We can only pray for the protection of women who go into demon-infested abortion mills and help them when their eyes are opened to the dreadful consequences of such a "choice."

In general, we must always be extremely careful to present the truth about abortion in a professional fashion to an abortion-minded woman, rather than trying to scare her out of an abortion by claiming that it is demonic or will cause infestation. Rather, sidewalk counselors and pregnancy care center workers must appeal to the woman's deepest maternal instincts and ask them to do the right thing, which they know in their hearts is what God wants of them. Even the arguments about possible physical and emotional injuries must be carefully presented so as not to sound like we are manipulating their emotions. The best sidewalk and pregnancy counselors offer these facts in the context of loving concern for the woman's total well-being, which is the only way to approach abortion-minded women. Only love defeats the desolation of the devil at those centers.

36. Do aborted women sometimes experience abortion as demonic?

At least one woman who wrote her testimony in a Yahoo "pre-abortion support forum" in January of 2007 expressed, with some agony, that her experience of abortion victimization was demonic. I share this testimony here anonymously, and we offer her our prayers:

> Before [the abortion] was done I thought of it as my "right" and really did not think of it as wrong, but when they started the process I knew I had touched on something really evil. I asked them to stop but they said "No," and the nurse held me down while the doctor did it. It felt like a rape by the devil. I tried to scream while the doctor was doing it, but no one even cared. I did not realize it would be that way, and I hate myself for asking them to kill him for me. I have nightmares about it all the time. Will it ever go away?

37. Why is it important for women who have had abortions to go through healing programs?

The primary reason for establishing post-abortion healing programs is that healing is a work of mercy. Truly, women who have experienced Christ's Mercy through post-abortion healing programs are much stronger, more mature and accepting of the truth about abortion than before they received healing. They often become the best advocates for life after their healing experience. The wounds of abortion need to be healed at many different levels because the human person is not just a psychological being; physical healing requires a doctor, emotional healing requires a therapist, and spiritual healing requires the spiritual resource of the Church. Post-abortion healing programs should address all levels of the human person, in order to effectively serve the needs of wounded women.

Another reason why women need post-abortion healing is that about 45% of the abortions in America are repeat abortions. Some women who never reconcile with the experience of the first abortion turn to abortion again thinking that it will justify the first one and somehow make them feel better about it. Without healing, they often fall into disordered lifestyles that lead them back to the abortion mill. Those who truly heal from abortion generally do not ever visit the abortion mill again. Post-abortion healing programs save babies by helping their mothers become whole once again.

To see a woman healed from abortion is one of the greatest joys of the pro-life movement. One time a woman called me wanting deliverance from demons. In the course of our conversation, she revealed that she had had an abortion, and I suspected that what she needed was post-abortion healing rather than true deliverance. I recommended that she go to a local program first and then come back to me if she felt that her demonic problems persisted. Within weeks, this valiant woman had been through a healing program and later on wrote to tell me that she felt 100% better and did not think that she needed deliverance. In fact, she had been delivered by the post-abortion healing!

38. What is our obligation as Christians to unborn babies in danger of abortion?

First and foremost, we recognize that the aborted baby is the most innocent of all victims of violent crimes and especially worthy of the Church's loving concern. No child should ever have to experience this type of violence, and as members of the Body of Christ, *we have a supreme obligation to rescue them and to be vigilant for the welfare of all unborn babies.* In such a cultural environment where unborn children have been completely deprived of the rights of personhood, 100% of babies are legally abort-able.

Never in history has there been such a dramatic and vulnerable child-protection situation. This modern evil has a claim on us as Christians. We are not detached observers who watch and let evil things destroy the innocent and indeed our very society. Pope John Paul II said that "if the right to life is not defended decisively as a condition for all other rights of the person, all other references to human rights remain deceitful and illusory."[58]

We are told in the parable of the sheep and goats[59] that Christ loves His "least brethren" in a special way, and that we will be judged according to how we treat Christ in the person of those who suffer. Our question should be: "What happens to *us* if we do not defend Christ's brothers and sisters who are being taken off to be killed in abortion mills?" Christ promised that all kinds of sinners and imperfect people will enter into the Kingdom of God with Him, but those who are "lukewarm" and do nothing in the face of such a clear moral imperative, He will simply "spew out of his mouth."[60]

39. What happens to the baby who is killed by such an evil as abortion?

Concerning the fate of aborted babies, we must grapple with our theological notions about baptism. There are only three forms of sacramental or quasi-sacramental baptism: by water, by blood and by desire. Aborted babies obviously do not qualify for *baptism by water*, since they do not meet the basic conditions for it: the pouring of water on the head and the pronunciation of the Trinitarian formula. Some think that *womb water* will suffice for a legitimate baptism simply because it is touching the baby! No! This does not meet the conditions of a valid baptism by water.

---

58 Cf. *Chrisifideles Laici*, 38 and his public address on February 14, 2001.

59 Matthew 25:31-46

60 Cf. Rev 3: 16

Others take the position that all aborted babies are martyrs and go to heaven because they have paid the ultimate price of shedding their blood. They cite the Holy Innocents as proof. However, this is not a strong theological view because the criterion for Christian martyrdom is the shedding of one's blood *for Christ* or being killed out of hatred *of the Church*. Aborted babies are killed violently for sure, but they are not generally killed under these conditions. The Church recognizes the martyrdom of the Holy Innocents precisely because they shed their blood for (in place of) the Christ Child, but abortion does not qualify in the same way. Babies are aborted as the result of a demonic evil that has become institutionalized in society, not as a deliberate persecution of the Church.

There are several positions that have been articulated by theologians in the past concerning the "baptism of desire" that are worth stating. A recent *Inside the Vatican* interview cited a theological text stating several positions of theologians on this issue over the centuries:

> Other emergency means of baptism for children dying without sacramental baptism, such as prayer and the desire of the parents or the Church (vicarious baptism of desire—Cajetan), or the attainment of the use of reason in the moment of death, so that the dying child can decide for or against God (baptism of desire—H. Klee), or suffering and death of the child as quasi-Sacrament (baptism of suffering—H. Schell), are indeed possible, but their actuality cannot be proved from Revelation.[61]

The article goes on to cite the recent document on Limbo issued by the International Theological Commission in which it was stated that "it must be clearly acknowledged that the Church does not have sure knowledge about the salvation of unbaptized

---

61   *Op. cit.*, Andrew Rabel, "Limbo: In or Out?" April 2007.

infants who die. She knows and celebrates the glory of the Holy Innocents, but the destiny of the generality of infants who die without Baptism has not been revealed to us, and the Church teaches and judges only with regard to what has been revealed. What we do positively know of God, Christ and the Church gives us grounds to hope for their salvation…."[62]

In addition to the above, another coherent Catholic position on the baptism of aborted babies is to say that *the desire of the Church* is a strong reason to hope for their salvation. This position has not been revealed to us in Scripture or Tradition but is a logical and common sense position. In the baptism of water, the parents and godparents display this same desire for their baby's salvation; it is not the conscious act or desire of the child. In the same way, the members of the pro-life movement are, in a very real sense, the *spiritual godparents* of these aborted children, especially when they are gathered in front of the places where the babies are being killed. Even when the biological parents have renounced their responsibility for the upbringing of the child, godparents can supply the desire of the Church for their salvation.

Archbishop Fulton J. Sheen's famous spiritual adoption prayer perhaps expresses this desire of the Church in its most tender terms:

> *Jesus, Mary and Joseph, we love you very much!*
> *We beg you to spare the life of the unborn child*
> *Whom we have spiritually adopted*
> *And who is in danger of abortion.*[63]

---

62   International Theological Commission, "The Hope of Salvation for Infants Who Die Without Being Baptized," April 20, 2007, n. 79.

63   This prayer has been attributed to Archbishop Fulton J. Sheen.

40. Can a baby be baptized *after* he is aborted?

There is hardly a more demonically-oriented idea and act than that of the so-called "baptism" of dead babies after the abortion has snuffed out their little lives. This practice is both a blasphemous mockery of the holy sacrament and preys upon the weakness of women who may choose a late-term abortion out of some misguided notion that their babies will be "saved" or sanctified by the act. Furthermore, since such an act could only be done on a late-term baby, it could have the further macabre effect of causing women to postpone abortions to such a point that the baby's body is large enough to "receive baptism." The act of pouring water on a corpse would not actually convey the sacrament to the baby (who has to be *alive* to receive it) and may actually be a demonic incentive for more women to kill their babies in this way. The late-term abortionist in Wichita, KS, George Tiller, offered this type of baptismal service to women, which even included the participation of a local Protestant minister. This practice is to be utterly and unequivocally condemned as a truly demonic evil.[64]

41. Should we "baptize" unborn babies who are being taken in to be aborted?

The answer to this question is a categorical "no." While well-intentioned, the attempt to "baptize" babies at a distance in a desperate gesture of compassion, or thwoing water in the direction of women going into killing centers, opens the pro-life movement to ridicule. As per Questions 39 and 40 above, these are not sacramentally valid ways to baptize.

The only "baptism" that is open to pro-lifers is that of the Church's desire as mentioned above. The desire itself is an act

---

64 Appendix A contains a picture of abortionist Tiller's "chaplain" and the "advertisement" that he included on his website justifying the blasphemous ceremony.

of faith of the people of God that places the babies squarely in the bosom of the Church's hope in Christ's Mercy and expresses with deepest tenderness the Church's love for those who suffer so unjustly. May God have mercy on them and on the souls of all those who perpetrate their deaths.

"Since we have these promises, beloved, let us purify ourselves from every defilement of flesh and spirit, and in the fear of God strive to fulfill our consecration perfectly" (2 Cor 7:1).

Appendix A

Abortion As "Sacrament"—In Their Own Words

The materials in this appendix attempt to make clear the demonic nature of those who practice or advocate abortion. These quotes do not mean that everyone who is in favor of abortion has similar diabolical ideas: indeed, there are many reasons why people are in favor of abortion, most of them just misguided. However, the shocking testimonies of some of the extreme advocates of baby-killing should help us all to see that we are dealing with human beings under the influence of "the principalities and powers, the rulers of this world of darkness."[65] The author urges all who read this appendix to pray for the salvation of the individuals cited below and for all who advocate abortion.

---

† Abortion is Worth Going to Hell For

Sidewalk counselor: "You can't go to heaven unrepentant, George; you are going to Hell."

Abortionist George Tiller: "Abortion is worth going to Hell for."

> — Conversation on the morning of January 22, 2003 outside **George Tiller's** third-trimester abortion mill, described in Operation Rescue West media advisory dated February 11, 2003.

---

65   Eph 6:12

† If Women Were In Charge

The seeds of goodness and truth and beauty, even as we gather here, are being sown.... If women had made the rules, if women had written the sacred texts, if women had been the architects of religion and state, sexuality would be understood as sacramental, so too would the act of love-making, — whether heterosexual or homosexual — so too would conception, miscarrying, and birth.

Abortion *would* be a sacrament if women were in charge. Abortion should be a sacrament even today. I suspect that for many women today, and for their spouses, lovers, families and communities, abortion is celebrated as such, an occasion of deep and serious and sacred meaning.

— **Carter Hayward, Episcopalian priest,** speaking at the ninth annual meeting of the National Abortion Federation (NAF), June 9-12, 1985, at the Westin Hotel in Boston, Massachusetts. Quoted in Andrew Scholberg. "The Abortionists Meet: 1985." *Primum Non Nocere* [newsletter of the American Section of the World Federation of Doctors Who Respect Human Life], Volume VI, Numbers 2 and 3, pages 1 through 6 [the abortionists in attendance cheered and applauded loudly when Hayward said the last couple of sentences].

† The "Holy Abortionist"

Abortion is a sacred rite that has been performed by women for centuries. The midwife, healer, shaman or witch is the holy abortionist. She has been hounded by christians for millennia. It is time for this witch-hunt to end!

With the help of the holy abortionist, in the form of the death goddess, the crone, or the medusa, we will overcome this new onslaught by the christian fanatics. Century after century, these zealots try to impose their feeble morality on women. They claim that god has sovereign power over issues of life and death.

This is far from the truth. Women as the goddess incarnate in all her forms and in particular in the shape of the hag, shrew, or fury who devours life in her gaping mouth with her sharp fangs, has sovereign power over issues of life and death. Let us not forget that when she decides her children are fated to die, so be it! . . . Like Lilith, she mercifully robs them of their breath. We are all on loan here and the death goddess must protect her own interests! No one can argue with the whirlwind who sweeps the doomed away! Her word is law!

Today we hope to invoke the wisdom and justice of the sacred abortionist, and in defense of women we scoff at these hysterical christians! All hope for an overpopulated planet is born in the darkness of her lethal grasp! Praise loudly the victorious destroyer of unwanted and unneeded children! She who has the right of jurisdiction owns the souls of this earthly tribe! ... With sickle in hand, she seizes the sated and weary souls of the damned!

These christians here today only make her job more difficult than it needs to be. Like a goblin-mother, she who suckles the stillborn babe also comforts the mad and possessed. . . . The nature of desire, the truth of life itself has always been death—the all-seeing one who demands responsibility from those who procreate and overpopulate this overburdened planet.

These misguided christians think they can strike a bargain with the grave, shriek at the whirlwind, bellow and screech at the all-devouring one. The fearful one, the holy abortionist is deaf to their pleading and will win in the end!

— **Nevada Kerr.** "Abortion As A Sacred Right," excerpted from *The Collected Sayings of Muad'Dib* by the Princess Irulan, found at (the truly sick website) www.churchofeuthanasia.org.

---

† A Sermon to Abortion Providers

I want to thank all of you who protect this blessing [of abortion]—who do this work every day: the health care providers, doctors, nurses, technicians, receptionists, who put your lives on the line to care for others (you are heroes—in my eyes, you are saints); the escorts and the activists; the lobbyists and the clinic defenders; all of you. You're engaged in holy work.

— **Rev. Katherine Ragsdale, Episcopalian priest.** Cited in the *American Spectator* article, "High Priestess of Abortion." May 8, 2009. http://spectator.org/archives/2009/05/08/high-priestess-of-abortion. [*Note:* Rev. Ragsdale is the first female president of Episcopal Divinity School in Cambridge, Massachusetts. She is openly lesbian and was once the chief of a liberal think tank monitoring the Religious Right. She is best known for her abortion rights advocacy through the Washington-based Religious Coalition for Reproductive Choice (RCRC).]

---

† God Rejoices in a Woman's Choice to Abort

After reading the 3 June article, "Pregnancy-loss Prayers," I found the text for Rachel's Tears[66] online and was sickened to

---

66 This refers to a 2009 resolution of the Episcopal Church USA called, "Rachel's Tears, Hannah's Hopes: Liturgies and Prayers for Healing from Loss Related to Childbearing and Childbirth." The liturgical ceremony includes a "Rite of Repentance and Reconciliation for an Abortion," to which Rev. Churchman objected.

discover that the rite for abortion is couched wholly in terms of sin and transgression. The Episcopal Church, by resolution, has long held that women have the freedom to choose an abortion. It is not considered a sin. That this new rite begins with the words, "I seek God's forgiveness . . ." and includes "God rejoices that you have come seeking God's merciful forgiveness . . . " is contrary to the resolution. Women should be able to mourn the loss of an aborted fetus without having to confess anything. God, unlike what the liturgy states, also rejoices that women facing unplanned pregnancies have the freedom to carefully choose the best option - birth, adoption or abortion - for themselves and their families. No woman makes this decision lightly or frivolously. But each needs the non-judgmental and non-coercive support of her faith community to make the best decision for her circumstances. The wording of this liturgy focuses solely on guilt and sin instead of the grief and healing that may accompany a very difficult but appropriate decision to terminate a pregnancy. If anyone is paying attention at the General Convention, this rite should not be approved.

— **Rev. Nina Churchman, Episcopalian priest.** Cited in: http://www.creativeminorityreport.com/June 24, 2009.

---

† A Major Blessing

Abortion is a major blessing, and a sacrament in the hands of women. . . . At the very crucible of the sacrament of abortion work is that some women have an abortion out of love for the baby, [some] out of love for the children they already have and are having a hard time feeding. They love what they are getting from their education and they know they can't stop it.

— **Patricia Baird-Windle, former owner of 3 abortuaries,** quoted in an August 29, 1999 interview with *Florida Today*, and in "The 'Sacrament' of Abortion: An Interview With a Retired Abortionist." *LifeSite Daily News*, August 31, 1999. [*Note:* Interestingly, during the interview in which Baird-Windle announced her retirement, but proudly acknowledged her responsibility in 65,000 abortions, she denounced the abortifacient drug, RU-486. "RU-486 is painful. Women have a great deal of pain and nausea and many visits to the clinic," she said].

---

† **Book:** *Abortion Is A Blessing*—**To A Radical Feminist**

The stories of the hundreds of women that I have counseled personally, and the thousands of women from all over the country that I have talked to on the phone, have resulted in my clear understanding that abortion is a positive thing, a cure, a blessing. I have become impatient not only with those religious zealots who tiresomely hiss "Murderers," but with those apologists who, while granting the right to abortion, insist that somehow a woman must feel guilt and remorse. I have come to suspect that the persons who refer to abortion as "a tragic option," or "a terrible alternative," hold allegiance not to women's freedom but to a male-dominated world gone by (p. 4). . . .

Birth control and abortion are our greatest steps forward in social and moral progress since we freed the slaves. A woman's right to control her own reproductive life is a blessing, a blessing for her and a blessing for society. There is no reason to be bashful or apologetic about supporting women's freedom to choose abortion; there is every reason to be ashamed of supporting a religion that opposes that freedom (p. 40). . . .

Male supremacists, fundamentalists, and the Catholic Church finally have met their match. Feminists will work until the freedom to choose abortion is extended to women everywhere (p. 49).

> — **Anne Nicol Gaylor, founder of the Freedom From Religion Foundation (FFRF).** *Abortion is a Blessing* [New York City: Psychological Dimensions, Inc.], 1975. Downloaded from the website of the FFRF at http://ffrf. org/books/AIAB/.

---

† We Are Goddesses—Life and Death is Our Decision

The issues that control freaks bring up – Is the fetus alive? – Is it morally right to kill? etc. – are non-issues. I don't think there's even a question for most of us that life is life, fully divine. The issue is: our religious creed is "Thou art Goddess." Do we mean it or not? Is it true or not? ... Are we willing to deny anyone else the right to interfere in our choices as Mother/Goddess about how we handle our sexuality and our fertility and our motherhood because we assume 100% responsibility for all of our actions and their consequences? Are we Goddess, or do we try in vain to abdicate the responsibility? (*Green Egg Magazine*, Vol. XXIV, No. 94, Mabon, 1991, p. 24)

> — **Tess Kolney, a member of the Gaian activist Church of All Worlds**, responding to "pagans" who claimed to be pro-life. Cited at: http://www.forerunner.com/champion/ X0003_Grist_for_the_Mills.html.

---

† Witch-Speak From a "Catholic" Feminist

There is no theological or scientific consensus on the beginning of human life. . . . The job of religious progressives is to clearly state that women are to be trusted, that women have and will continue to make just and person-enhancing choices about the quality of life — beginning with the quality of women's lives.... We need to develop a society where women's reproductive choice is normative and where reproductive options are considered a human right....

Women's right to choose is what I, as a Catholic, dare to call sacramental.... Reproductive choice is a sacred trust and women are more than equal to the task. Bringing this to public expression, "praising our choices" as poet Marge Piercy has said, is something that a just society will celebrate as sacramental.

Second, fathers' rights need to be considered, but they are far down the ethical ladder when it comes to who decides about abortion.... I mean especially lesbian mothers who have the right, not the privilege, to use reproductive technology to choose to have children by self-insemination (we no longer consider it "artificial") ... Third, in a just society every health maintenance organization, every insurance company and every group practice will include abortion as a regular part of its services without the need to agonize, specialize and ostracize when the word is mentioned.... It reminds me of the doctors who have chosen not to treat people with AIDS. In a just society, such doctors would, as Dr. Mervyn Silverman suggested, get another kind of work....

— **Mary E. Hunt.** "Abortion in a Just Society." *Conscience* (newsletter of "Catholics" for a Free Choice), July/August 1988 [Volume IX, Number 4], pages 9 to 12. [*Note:* Mary Hunt is a feminist theologian who is **co-founder and co-director of the Women's Alliance for Theology, Ethics and Ritual (WATER)** in Silver Spring, Maryland, and an **advisor to the Women's Ordination Conference**. She is a former member of the "Catholics" for a Free Choice Board of Directors. She claims to be a Roman Catholic active in the women-church movement, and lives in Silver Spring, Maryland, with her partner, Diann L. Neu, and their daughter, Catherine Fei Min Hunt-Neu.]

---

† Abortion is a Sacrifice to Artemis

When my turn came [for an abortion] I stretched out on the table, feet in the stirrups, ready to let my little darling go. . . . I realized that, even if my head and my heart accepted the loss, my uterus still saw it as a mortal threat and was protesting with all its strength in an effort to protect its little lodger. I was very proud of my uterus for doing its job so well! . . . The next day life went back to normal. But curiously, several friends I met asked me: "What's going on with you? You're so radiant today, you're absolutely glowing." What's going on is that I've just had an abortion and lived an *impossible love* and accomplished a great reconciliation with myself. But it was my secret and my gift (pp. 98-99).

. . . Christianity taught us to be ashamed of our bodies, of some of our emotions, of femininity, and many therapists are busy treating the embarrassment that lingers in the subconscious, even when we think we've rid ourselves of old religious strictures (p. 104). . . .

When an abortion is necessary, not only should there be no shame, but there should be a new consensus that to have a child who cannot adequately be cared for is shameful (p. 106).

. . . The same quality allows us to visualize a world of increasing respect for children, a world in which one can occasionally resort to abortion when it is necessary to sacrifice the fetus to a higher cause, namely, the love of children and the refusal to see them suffer. Abortion as a sacrifice to Artemis. Abortion as a sacrament — for the gift of life to remain pure. . . . One must preserve in one's self . . . an intact strength, inviolable and radically feminine; this is the Artemesian part of the anima which guards the untamed zone of our psyche, without which we risk becoming over-domesticated human beings, too easily touchable (p. 107). . . .

— **Ginette Paris.** *The Sacrament of Abortion,* translated from French by Joanna Mott, Dallas: Spring Publications, 1992. [Emphasis in original.] For a more complete set of quotes from this hideous book, please visit the web page: http://www.forerunner.com/champion/X0004_Paris_Sacrament.html.

---

† Abortion Grieving Rituals

The lights were low, and Native American flute music played softly. A counselor held the woman's hand, whispering words of comfort as she began to surface from a guided meditation. Then the doctor showed the woman a covered silver bowl that held the tiny remains of her six-week pregnancy. She curled her fingers around his, and her face, now damp with tears, softened as he began their ceremony of letting go.

"We ask your blessing, in the name of love," Curtis Boyd, M.D. [retired abortionist in Albuquerque, NM], began softly. Before becoming a doctor, Boyd was a foot-washing Baptist minister in rural East Texas. He left the fold but took with him an abiding faith in the power of ceremony to heal, honor, and comfort.

"Women, because of what they are bombarded with in the media and by anti-abortion groups, get the message that what they are doing is wrong and that they are bad people," Boyd says,

"A ceremony says the woman is a good and caring person who made the best decision she could under difficult circumstances. It also gives her a way to honor the fetus, to be aware of her grief, and to express her loss."

This particular afternoon, in the soft light of the surgery room, Boyd concluded the ceremony with a prayer: "We ask that you honor this woman's courage, and bless her and her family as they move forward in their lives."

> — **Patricia O'Connor, abortion mill counselor,** quoted from *New Age* magazine, March/April, 1998, p. 17, and cited in "More Grist From the Abortion Mills," http://www.fore-runner.com/champion/X0003_Grist_for_the_Mills.html.

---

† The "Sacred Ground" of an Abortuary

The *Albany Times-Union* reported that religious leaders in favor of abortion gathered with three dozen others in Schenectady, NY on Jan 23, 2008 to "bless" an 18,000-square-foot abortion center in support of the *Roe v. Wade* ruling, the Supreme Court decision that legalized abortion nationwide. The various religious leaders in attendance participated in the ceremony with religious language and ritual actions. The following are excerpts from the article:

> *The Rev. Larry Phillips* of Schenectady's Emmanuel-Friedens Church declared the ground "sacred and holy . . . where women's voices and stories are welcomed, valued and affirmed; sacred ground where women are treated with dignity, supported in their role as moral decision-makers . . . sacred ground where the violent voices of hatred and oppression are quelled." *The Rev. Abby Norton-Levering* led the group in prayers for the center's doctors and staff. "We pray that you

will make this a place of safety and give a sense of sanctuary," she said.

Rabbi Matt Cutler of Temple Gates of Heaven blew the shofar as "a renewal of commitment to keep reproductive rights in the hands of women."

The Rev. Bill Levering, senior pastor of First Reformed Church of Schenectady, said the right to privacy is endowed by God. "There are some decisions that are left to the individual. Even God respects the right of privacy. We make women into children when we say they cannot control their own bodies," Levering said.

Phillips led everyone outside where they laid their hands on the brick and limestone as the minister declared, "This is sacred ground."

— http://blogs.timesunion.com/localpolitics/?p=1030.

---

† The Clergyman From Hell

Gracious and loving God, be with all of those brave souls who make abortion possible. Hold them in your loving embrace and keep them safe — doctors, nurses, clinic staff, administrators, janitors and counselors and receptionists — all those who labor to provide abortions to those in need. Bless them and keep them safe from harm and harassment, intimidation and fear. Hear us, O God, as we lift up our voices to you, and say in all your many names. Amen.

— **Rev. Matthew Westfox, United Church of Christ**, prayer recited at an abortion clinic prayer vigil on the weekend of October 16-18, 2009, entitled, "Weekend of Prayerful Affirmation and Action for the Safety of Clinic Workers," sponsored by the Religious Coalition for Reproductive Choice (RCRC).

---

† Satan's Benediction: "Let the Spirit of Dr. Tiller Live On"

With the murder of Dr. Tiller, our movement, our world, lost a great man. We mourn his loss, but we remember that his spirit lives on. That any time a doctor or a nurse or a clinic practitioner goes to work to provide abortion care to those in need, the spirit of Dr. Tiller lives on. That any time an elected official submits a bill or casts a vote in favor of justice, in favor of clinic defense, in favor of access, that the spirit of Dr. Tiller lives on. That every time we come to a vigil and say, "No more violence, no more killings; clinic workers must work in peace," the spirit of Dr. Tiller lives on. That every time we give of our hearts, through gifts of time, or money, or energy or volunteerism, we make it possible for women to have access to needed services, and the spirit of Dr. Tiller lives on. By doing all we can to make abortions accessible and safe, the spirit of Dr. Tiller lives on. . . .

Gracious and loving God, let your strength flow through all of us. Let all of us honor the memory of this great man, and keep his spirit with us as we work for justice, work for access, and work together to make sure that no doctor, no administrator, no clinic worker is ever murdered again.

— **Rev. Matthew Westfox** gave this "benediction" at a Planned Parenthood-sponsored rally for murdered late-term abortionist, George Tiller, on June 1, 2009 in Union Square, NYC. Cited at: http://fratres.wordpress.com/2009/10/13/satanic-prayer-vigils-that-they-might-abort-children-in-peace/.

† Baptize Your Baby—*After* Killing Her

The website of the former late-term abortionist, George Tiller, contained a macabre portrayal of the depths to which some in the industry would stoop to mollify the innate human revulsion towards the practice of abortion. The "services" offered by abortionist Tiller and his clinic's "chaplain" are truly gruesome. The following was reproduced from the website of the former abortion mill:

> Many patients request a remembrance of their baby to take home with them. The following lists items and services that some of our previous patients have found helpful in their emotional recovery. Everyone approaches this experience with their own unique emotional, spiritual, and cultural background. There is no right way or wrong way, just "your way." Once the process of healing has begun, you may want to consider a token of the precious time you and your baby had together. All of these features of our program will be discussed with you while you are with us:

- Viewing your baby after delivery

- Holding your baby after delivery

- Photographs of your baby

- Baptism of your baby, with or without a certificate

- Footprints and handprints of your baby

- Certificate of premature miscarriage

- Cremation

- An urn for ashes

- Arrangement of burial in either Wichita or your home state

- Arrangement of amniocentesis/autopsy

- Medical photographs and x-rays for your health care professional

Grief is a very complex emotion which is expressed in many different ways. We will attempt to accommodate your individual requests to the very best of our abilities.

Transcript of the audio recording of Dr. Tiller in his advertisement of the above services:

If you wish to see the baby, we call this an identification and separation encounter.[67] About 2-3 hours after you deliver and after the twilight anesthesia has worn off, so that you will remember the process, we will bring the baby to you either at the bedside or we will go to our quiet room and we will bring the baby to you there. During this encounter we will describe to you what's right with your baby, we will identify what's wrong with your baby. You may hold the baby. We can take pictures of you and the family holding the baby, if you wish, and that is not an uncommon request. The identification/separation encounter may be very brief, five or ten minutes. It may even take less than that. Or the identification/separation encounter may involve 2 or 3 hours of bonding with the baby - the identification that this is your baby and you have had a delivery. We understand beyond a

---

67 Tiller is talking here about "bonding" with the baby after she has been murdered in a late-term abortion. The "delivery" he speaks of is the killing procedure whereby a drug is injected into the baby's heart to instantly kill her. A fully-formed baby can be "delivered" stillborn and given back to the mother for some sick attempt at "identification" and grieving.

shadow of a doubt that the *difficult* part of this process is not the premature delivery of the stillborn. We understand that the *easy* part of this process is the premature delivery of the stillborn. The difficult part of the process is saying goodbye to the relationship that you have with your baby - saying goodbye to the hopes and the dreams that you have for this - you have placed this baby in your life someplace and you simply have to start the process of saying goodbye.

When you have finished your support - when you have finished your identification encounter - you will separate from the baby by giving the baby to us, and you will begin the process of saying goodbye on a long-term basis, and you will begin your journey into growth, recuperation, recovery, and healing.

Dr. Tiller's Chaplain, Rev. George Gardner, had his own section on the website too:

Meet Our Chaplain: George Gardner

The Chaplaincy program is designed to bring spiritual resources to those who come to the Clinic for help and assistance. Spiritually, abortion is acceptable in ten of the world's religions, and in Christianity, many denominations affirm and uphold the right of a woman to make the choice of abortion.

The Chaplaincy program works with people from all religious backgrounds as well as those who are not a part of a spiritual tradition. The program offers individual counseling, group counseling, and the celebration of spiritual sacraments such as baptism of the stillborn fetus and blessings for the aborted fetus. The program works with many different religions and is prepared to do, or arrange for, religious services from any spiritual religion.

The services of Women's Health Care Services is a coordinated effort so that every patient and significant other can experience the healing of body, mind and spirit.

— **The three items in the above section** are taken from the pro-life website: www.dr-tiller.com which reproduces the above audio track that was posted on the original website of the abortionist: www.drtiller.com. The pro-life website contains many more expressions of depravity from the abortion industry.

---

† **The following "prayer services" to justify the killing of a baby were composed by Diann L. Neu. The first two are currently published by "Catholics" for a Free Choice.**

Liturgy for Seeking Wisdom

Background

This liturgy will help a woman decide whether to bring her pregnancy to term or to have an abortion.

Centering

Play soothing instrumental music quietly in the background.

Candle Lighting

Light candle, absorb its power, pray.

Prayer

Gracious and loving Holy Wisdom, fill me with wisdom that I may see clearly the choice that I need to make.

Bless me and comfort me with your Spirit.

Visualization

* See yourself walking on a path through the woods. You are walking into the future. At the end of this path, see yourself in ten years if you decide to bring this pregnancy to term. (Pause for three minutes and listen to yourself.)

* Now begin again. (Pause fifteen seconds.) See another path through the woods. Walk along this path. At the end of this path see yourself in ten years if you do not bring this pregnancy to term. (Pause for three minutes and experience what this is like.)

* After you have visualized these two pathways, find a cozy room with a comfortable chair. Sit in this chair and think about what you have seen. (Pause for as long as you like).

Reflection

Sit and watch the candle burn, write down your thoughts in a journal and/or share your insights.

Closing

Wisdom comes when we reflect on our life and make choices based on honesty and truth. Wisdom lives within us. Listen to her. Trust her. Talk to her whenever you need to. She is your friend.

Song[68]

"i found god in myself"

> *for colored girls who have considered suicide/ when the rainbow is enuf.*
>
> *i found god in myself, i found god in myself and I loved her fiercely, i loved her fiercely,*
>
> *i found god in myself.*

Blow out the candle when you are finished. Do something comforting, for example, drink a cup of tea or take a warm shower.

Liturgy of Affirmation for Making a Difficult Decision

Background

This liturgy affirms that a woman has made a good and holy decision. It provides strength and healing after making a difficult decision. It brings closure to an often intense and emotional process. It is intended to be celebrated with friends.

Gathering

The celebrant invites friends, and if appropriate the partner, to gather in a circle. She welcomes them and introduces the liturgy.

Song

A favorite, comforting song, one that the woman likes.

---

68 All punctuation and orthography in original.

Prayer

Blessed are you, Holy One, for your presence with _____ (name of woman).

Praised be you, Mother and Father God, that you have given your people the power of choice. We are saddened that the life circumstances of _____ (woman's name or, if appropriate, woman's name and her partner's name) are such that she has had to choose to terminate her pregnancy. Such a choice is never simple. It is filled with pain and hurt, with anger and questions, but also with integrity and strength. We rejoice in her attention to choice.

Our beloved sister has made a very hard choice. We affirm her and support her in her decision. We promise to stand with her in her ongoing life.

Blessed are you, Holy One, for your presence with her.

Reading

Choose a poem, reading, or scripture verse that captures the message of the liturgy.

Sharing

The celebrant invites the woman (and her partner) to speak about her (their) decision to have an abortion. If there is a symbolic gesture that expresses her (their) feelings such as sprinkling flower petals, or sharing dried flowers, invite her (them) to incorporate.

Blessing of _____ *(name of woman)*

_____ , we love you very deeply. As a sign of our affirmation of you and of your choice, we give you this bowl and this oil. Oil soothes the bones that are weary from making a difficult decision. Oil strengthens and heals. Oil…(add sentences that reflect what the woman spoke in her story). We bless you with this oil. (Each person takes oil from the bowl and anoints the woman's hands, face, feet, neck, shoulders and/or head. Each closes the blessing by embracing her.) _____ (name of woman), the bowl is a tangible symbol of this day. When times are difficult — and such days come to each of us — look at this bowl and remember our love for you.

Closing song

A blessing song like the following closes the liturgy.

"Blessing Song," from the album *Circling Free*, © 1983 by Marsie Silvestro

> *Bless you my sister, bless you on your way*
> *You have roads to roam before you're home*
> *And winds to speak your name.*
>
> *So go gently my sister let courage be your song*
> *You have words to say in your own way*
> *and stars to light your night.*
>
> *And if ever you grow weary and your heart song has no refrain*
> *Just remember we'll be waiting to raise you up again.*
>
> *And we'll bless you our sister, bless you in our way*
> *And we'll welcome home all the life you've known and softly*
> *speak your name.*
>
> *And we'll welcome home all the self you own*
> *and softly speak your name*
> *Bless you my sister, bless you on your way.*

— Cited at: www.catholicsforchoice.org/topics/abortion/do cuments/2000youarenotalone_000.pdf.

A Litany of Challenge

Filled with the fullness of this day, with the stories of our sisters, with the bread of our community.... Let us go forth ...

To stand, sit, cry, pray with women making reproductive choices, especially the difficult choice for abortion.

To speak to legislators, family members, and friends of our support for women's decisions.

To challenge our churches, synagogues, and holy congregations to affirm women as moral agents.

To encourage ministers, rabbis, priests and counselors to counsel women on free choice.

To the city centers and country corners to tell women that all of their choices, including their choice for abortion, are holy and healthy.

In the name of the holy one, God of our mothers and God/ess of our fathers, to bring about justice.

Song

"Be Not Afraid"

> — The three items in the above section were composed by **Diann L. Neu.** The "Litany of Challenge" was part of a "prayer service," entitled "Praise Our Choices, Lift Our Voices," held on November 10, 1989 at the Reflecting Pool/ Lincoln Memorial in Washington, DC, to "celebrate the Rally to Mobilize for Women's Lives" (known more accurately by pro-lifers as the "March for Death"). The "service" was co-written by three feminist activists: Diann Neu; Rabbi Lynne Landsberg, the Associate Director of the Religious

Action Center of Reform Judaism; and Mary Jane Patterson, Director of the Washington Office of the Presbyterian Church, USA. [*Note:* Diann Neu is a feminist liturgist and psychotherapist and the **co-director of WATER, the Women's Alliance for Theology, Ethics and Ritual**. She lives with her partner, Mary E. Hunt and their daughter, Catherine Fei Min Hunt-Neu, in Silver Spring, MD.]

Appendix B

Scripture Passages Concerning Blood and the Precious Blood of Jesus

All Scripture quotes are taken from The New American Bible, *1970 edition.*

Abel's blood cries out

Genesis 4:8-11

Cain said to his brother Abel, "Let us go out in the field." When they were in the field, Cain attacked his brother Abel and killed him. Then the Lord asked Cain, "Where is your brother Abel?" He answered, "I do not know. Am I my brother's keeper?" The Lord then said: "What have you done! Listen: Your brother's blood cries out to me from the soil! Therefore you shall be banned from the soil that opened its mouth to receive your brother's blood from your hand."

Blood is sacred—the covenant with Noah

Genesis 9:3-6

Every creature that is alive shall be yours to eat; I give them all to you as I did the green plants. Only flesh with its lifeblood still in it you shall not eat. For your own lifeblood, too, I will demand an accounting; from every animal I will demand it, and from man in regard to his fellow man I will demand an accounting for human life. If anyone sheds the blood of man, by man shall his blood be shed; for in the image of God has man been made.

The blood of the Paschal Lamb on the doorposts and lintels

Exodus 12:5-7. 11-13

The lamb must be a year old male and without blemish....You shall keep it until the fourteenth day of this month, and then, with the whole assembly of Israel present, it shall be slaughtered during the evening twilight. They shall take some of its blood and apply it to the two doorposts and the lintel of every house in which they partake of the lamb. That same night they shall eat its roasted flesh with unleavened bread and bitter herbs. . . . it is the Passover of the Lord. For on this same night I will go through Egypt, striking down every first-born of the land, both man and beast, and executing judgment on all the gods of Egypt—I, the Lord! But the blood will mark the houses where you are. Seeing the blood, I will pass over you; thus, when I strike the land of Egypt, no destructive blow will come upon you.

Moses sprinkles the people with blood

Exodus 24:5-8

Then, having sent certain young men of the Israelites to offer holocausts and sacrifice young bulls as peace offerings to the Lord, Moses took half of the blood and put it in large bowls; the other half he splashed on the altar. Taking the book of the covenant, he read it aloud to the people, who answered, "All that the Lord has said, we will heed and do." Then he took the blood and sprinkled it on the people saying, "This is the blood of the covenant which the Lord has made with you in accordance with all these words of his."

Solomon offers blood sacrifice in the Temple

1 Kings 8:62-63

The king and all Israel with him offered sacrifices before the Lord. Solomon offered as peace offerings to the Lord twenty-two thousand oxen and one hundred and twenty thousand sheep. Thus the king and all the Israelites dedicated the temple of the Lord.

The sacredness of blood

Leviticus 17:11

Since the life of a living body is in its blood, I have bade you put it on the altar, so that atonement may thereby be made for your own lives, because it is the blood, as the seat of life, that makes atonement.

David offers blood sacrifice to stop a pestilence

2 Samuel 24:17 and 25

When David saw the angel who was striking the people, he said to the Lord, "It is I who have sinned; it is I, the shepherd, who have done wrong. But these are sheep; what have they done? Punish me and my kindred" . . . Then David built an altar there to the Lord, and offered holocausts and peace offerings. The Lord granted relief to the country, and the plague was checked in Israel.

The Sacred Heart of Jesus

John 19:33-34 and 36-37

When they came to Jesus and saw that he was already dead, they did not break his legs. One of the soldiers thrust a lance into his side, and immediately blood and water flowed out . . . These events took place for the fulfillment of Scripture: "Break none of his bones." There is still another Scripture passage which says: "They shall look on him whom they have pierced."

Christ's Blood breaks down the wall of separation

Ephesians 2:13-14

But now in Christ Jesus you who were once far off have been brought near through the blood of Christ. It is he who is our peace, and who made the two of us one by breaking down the barrier of hostility that kept us apart.

Christ's Blood cleanses consciences

Hebrews 9:11-14

In the performance of their service, the priests used to go into the outer tabernacle constantly, but only the high priest went into the inner one, and that but once a year, with the blood which he offered for himself and for the sins of the people. . . . But when Christ came as high priest of the good things which have come to be, he entered once for all into the sanctuary, passing through the greater and more perfect tabernacle not made by hands, that is, not belonging to this creation. He entered, not with the blood of goats and calves, but with his own blood, and achieved eternal redemption. For if the blood of goats and bulls and the sprinkling of a heifer's ashes can sanctify those who are defiled so that their flesh is cleansed, how much more will the blood of Christ, who through the eternal spirit offered himself up unblemished to God, cleanse our consciences from dead works to worship the living God.

Christ's Blood makes us confident to approach God

Heb 10:19-22

Brothers, since the blood of Jesus assures our entrance into the sanctuary by the new and living path he has opened for us ... and since we have a great priest who is over the house of God, let us draw near in utter sincerity and absolute confidence, our hearts sprinkled clean from the evil which lay on our conscience, and our bodies washed in pure water.

The Blood of Christ is more eloquent than the blood of Abel

Hebrews 12:22-24

You have drawn near to Mount Zion and to the city of the living God, the heavenly Jerusalem, to myriads of angels in festal gathering, to the assembly of the firstborn enrolled in heaven, to God the judge of all, to the spirits of just men made perfect, to Jesus, the mediator of a new covenant, and to the sprinkled blood which speaks more eloquently than that of Abel.

Purified by Christ's Blood

1 Peter 1:1-2

Peter, an apostle of Jesus Christ ... to men chosen according to the foreknowledge of God the Father, consecrated by the Spirit to a life of obedience to Jesus Christ and purification with his blood. Favor and peace be yours in abundance.

Jesus the spotless lamb

1 Peter 1:18-20

Realize that you were delivered from the futile way of life your fathers handed on to you, not by any diminishable sum of silver or gold, but by Christ's blood beyond all price: the blood of a spotless, unblemished lamb chosen before the world's foundation and revealed for your sake in these last days.

The cleansing power of Christ's Blood

1 John 1:7

But if we walk in light, as he is in light, we have fellowship with one another, and the blood of his Son Jesus cleanses us from all sin.

Three witnesses: the Spirit, the water and the blood

1 John 5:5-8

Who, then, is conqueror of the world? The one who believes that Jesus is the Son of God. Jesus Christ it is who came through water and blood—not in water only, but in water and in blood. It is the Spirit who testifies to this, and the Spirit is truth. Thus there are three that testify, the Spirit and the water and the blood—and these three are of one accord.

Freed of our sins by Christ's Blood

Revelation 1:5-6

Jesus Christ the faithful witness, the first-born from the dead and the ruler of the kings of earth. To him who loves us and freed us from our sins by his own blood, who made us a royal nation of priests in the service of his God and Father—to him be glory and power forever and ever! Amen.

Appendix C
Other Articles on Demonic Abortion

The following two articles appeared in my weekly e-newsletter, Spirit and Life, *in 2007 and have been reprinted and translated into several languages.*

Abortion: The Devil's Masterpiece

Friday, August 3, 2007

A few weeks ago I visited Leroy Carhart's partial birth abortion mill in Omaha, NE and beheld for a few uncomfortable moments a totally repulsive center of human wickedness. Just looking at the dilapidated former car repair garage turned into baby-killing factory and the squalor of the entire surrounding area, I could not help but notice that the evil of abortion degrades everything that it touches. Abortion is not only a social plague; it is also the spiritual negation of God's entire plan for man's happiness and eternal welfare. Whenever God says "Yes" to life and fertility, the devil yells a resounding "No!"

Abortion's spiritual power is its perfect violation of all the commandments. First of all, most abortions are the result of sins against the sixth or ninth commandments (adultery/fornication/lust). Abortion is certainly a sin against the fifth commandment prohibiting murder. Likewise, it violates the third commandment because the vast majority of babies are killed on abortion's heaviest business days, Saturdays (the Sabbath). Abortion is also a reversal of the fourth commandment where father and mother "dishonor" the child in the most heinous way and, in doing so, curse the holiness of God (second commandment) which is manifested in the only creature made in His "image and like-ness." As a false religion, abortion is a violation of the first commandment forbidding the worship of any other gods but the Lord, and this religion is undoubtedly fed through a highly sophisticated system of falsehoods and deceits (eighth commandment) which lead women into the abortion chambers.

Furthermore, abortion literally steals (seventh commandment) both our personal and national futures by depriving us of children! Anyone concerned about the present immigration issue should remember that the presence of more than forty million Hispanic immigrants in this country tracks the destruction of 47 million of our own children by abortion since the *Roe* death decision. The saying, "nature abhors a vacuum" is as true in demographics as it is in physics. Finally, the tenth commandment (coveting our neighbor's goods) is about the capital sin of greed, the very thing that drives so many of the abortionists to do the killing work. Abortionists often claim to hate abortion, but they love the money behind it.

Abortion is like a huge spiritual vortex of sin, pulling people into it, and even the Church can be compromised by this evil, too. Most of the sins listed above are sins of commission, but the Church's sins are generally sins of omission which abortion inspires—the terrible silence of the clergy on this topic, heretical "Catholic" politicians who are never disciplined by bishops, the easy justification of abortion by Catholic educators, the moral compromise by Catholic medical personnel on abortifacient contraception and sterilizations, etc. I am sure the devil just laughs and pats himself on the back when he sees the Church, that has the spiritual power to undo "all his work and all his empty promises," sitting back and pretending that abortion is a non-issue.

All of this is to point out that abortion is a spiritual power that negates God's plan for love, life and the family. It not only destroys bodies but destroys souls, which from the point of view of eternity, represents the devil's greatest masterpiece of evil.

The "Sacrament" of Abortion

Friday, August 10, 2007

The standard Catholic description of a real Sacrament is that it is an "efficacious sign instituted by Christ to give grace." The "sign" is whatever the particular Sacrament is meant to convey: Baptism—cleansing from sin, Eucharist—union with Christ, Penance—forgiveness of sins, etc. "Efficacious" means that it actually produces the effect it signifies, and it "gives grace" as sort of a conduit of divine life into our souls. A Catholic Sacrament is holy in itself and does not need a holy person to administer it; and on the basis of the Sacrament's innate holiness, the children of the Church are sanctified and in turn sanctify the world in which we live.

The demonic "sacrament" of abortion has the same characteristics as a real Sacrament except that it reverses any concept of holiness and perverts its meaning. This is because the devil always mimics God's plan to communicate His life to us and does everything he can to draw us away from that life. In this case, abortion is a "sign" that points to death; it is "efficacious" in that it brings death through bodily destruction; it "destroys grace" in that each act of abortion is a mortal sin that seduces and corrupts all of those who take part in it.

Furthermore, abortionists, witches and Satanists put their "faith" in the "sacrament" of abortion. Don't take my word for it. In a 1999 *LifeSite* interview, retired abortionist Patricia Baird-Windle, self-professed wiccan (witch), actually said, "Abortion is a major blessing, and a sacrament in the hands of women. . . . At the very crucible of the sacrament of abortion work is that some women have an abortion out of love for the baby, [some] out of love for the children they already have and are having a hard time feeding." Rarely am I shocked by what abortion apologists say, but this perverse logic leaves me utterly speechless. It shouldn't surprise me, though; Ms. Baird-Windle claims responsibility for 65,000 abortions in the three death centers that she owned.

There's more. An Episcopal "priestess," Carter Hayward, said,[69] "Abortion would be a sacrament if women were in charge. Abortion should be a sacrament even today. I suspect that for many women today, and for their spouses, lovers, families and communities, abortion is celebrated as such, an occasion of deep and serious and sacred meaning." No comment is really necessary here.

Let us never pretend that abortion is just a social or political phenomenon that has to be voted out of office to be defeated. We must do everything we can to restore legal protection to our most innocent citizens, but our battle against the devil will not be won at the polls. It will be won on our knees before the Lord and on our feet before the centers of death. More than ever we need men and women of tested holiness who are willing to fight the spiritual battle for the lives of God's precious babies and the souls of their mothers and fathers. Even abortionists like Baird-Windle are caught up in a demonic religion which can be challenged and defeated by those of us who belong to the true Church of Christ, the only spiritual power strong enough to defeat the "sacrament" of abortion.

---

69 See full quote and citation from Rev. Hayward in Appendix A.

Short Bibliography of Best Pro-Life Resources

Books

Randy Alcorn, *Pro-Life Answers to Pro-Choice Arguments* (Multnomah), 2009.

Randy Alcorn, *Does the Birth Control Pill Cause Abortions?* (Eternal Perspective Ministries), 2004.

Francis Beckwith, *Politically Correct Death: Answering Arguments for Abortion Rights* (Baker Books), 1998.

William Brennan, *Dehumanizing the Vulnerable: When Word Games Take Lives* (Loyola), 1995.

Brian Clowes, *The Facts of Life* (Human Life International), 2001.

Brian Clowes, *Pro-Life CD Library* (Human Life International), 2008.

Brian Clowes, *Seminarian Pro-Life Handbook* (Human Life International), 2010.

Mark Crutcher, *Lime 5: Exploited by Choice* (Life Dynamics), 1996.

Mark Crutcher, *On Message: The Pro-Life Handbook* (Life Dynamics), 2005.

Eugene F. Diamond, MD, *A Catholic Guide to Medical Ethics* (Linacre), 2001.

Eamonn Keane, *The Brave New World of Therapeutic Cloning* (Human Life International), 2001.

John F. Kippley, *Birth Control and Christian Discipleship* (Couple to Couple League), 1994.

Donald De Marco and Benjamin D. Wiker, *Architects of the Culture of Death* (Ignatius), 2004.

Rev. Paul B. Marx, *The Death Peddlers* (Human Life International), 1998.

Pontifical Council for the Family, *Lexicon: Ambiguous and debatable terms regarding family life and ethical questions* (Human Life International), 2006.

Pro-Life Action League, *Sharing the Pro-Life Message*, 2009.

David Reardon, *Victims and Victors* (Acorn), 2000.

Stephen Schwarz, *The Moral Question of Abortion* (Loyola), 1990.

Janet E. Smith, *Why Humanae Vitae Was Right: A Reader*, (Ignatius), 1993.

John and Barbara Willke, *Abortion: Questions and Answers* (Hayes), 2003.

Church Documents

Bioethics and Sexual Ethics

Congregation for the Doctrine of the Faith, *Declaration on Certain Questions Concerning Sexual Ethics*, 1975.

Congregation for the Doctrine of the Faith, *Donum Vitae*, 1987.

Pontifical Academy for Life, "Statement on the So-Called 'Morning After Pill,'" 2000.

Congregation for the Doctrine of the Faith, *Dignitas Personae*, 2007.

Marriage and Family

Pope Pius XI, *Casti Connubii*, 1930.

Pope Paul VI, *Humanae Vitae*, 1968.

Pope John Paul II, *Familiaris Consortio*, 1982.

Pontifical Council for the Family, "Charter on the Rights of the Family," 1983.

Pope John Paul II, *Letter to Families*, 1994.

Pontifical Council for the Family, *The Truth and Meaning of Human Sexuality*, 1995.

Population Control

Pope John XXIII, *Mater et Magistra*, 1961.

Pope Paul VI, *Populorum Progressio*, 1967.

Pontifical Council for the Family, *Ethical and Pastoral Dimensions of Population Trends*, 1994.

Respect for Life

Congregation for the Doctrine of the Faith, *Declaration on Procured Abortion*, 1974.

Pope John Paul II, *Evangelium Vitae*, 1995.

Organizations

40 Days for Life (prayer and fasting to end abortion), www.40daysforlife.com.

American Life League (comprehensive pro-life resource), www.all.org.

Association of Large Families of America (ALFA), www.fourormore.org.

Association of Pro-Life Physicians, www.prolifephysicians.org.

Catholic Family and Human Rights Institute (called C-Fam, pro-life lobbying at the United Nations), www.c-fam.org.

Catholic Medical Association, www.cathmed.org.

Center for Bioethical Reform (GAP—Genocide Awareness Project), www.abortionNO.org.

Helpers of God's Precious Infants (pro-life prayer vigils at abortion mills), www.helpersbrooklynny.org.

Human Life International (HLI—pro-life missionaries to the world), www.hli.org.

HLI America (fighting the "big lie" of contraception), www.hliamerica.org.

Life Decisions International (boycotting Planned Parenthood), www.fightpp.org.

Life Dynamics (investigating the abortion industry), www.lifedynamics.com.

Live Action (exposing Planned Parenthood's criminal activity), www.liveaction.org.

Pharmacists for Life International (pro-life pharmacy news and information), www.pfli.org.

Priests for Life, www.priestsforlife.org.

Pro-Life Action League (Chicago-based activist organization), www.prolifeaction.org.

Society for the Protection of Unborn Children (called SPUC, oldest continuous pro-life organization in the world, based in London), www.spuc.org.uk.

Vida Humana Internacional (HLI's Hispanic Division), www.vidahumana.org.

Videos/DVDs

99 Balloons (YouTube)

Baby Steps (American Life League)

The Biology of Prenatal Development (National Geographic)

Choice Blues (Center for Bio-Ethical Reform)

Honest Answers (Selena Lin, Heritage House)

In the Womb Collection (National Geographic)

Lila Rose's videos exposing on Planned Parenthood (Live Action Films)

Silent Scream (American Portrait Films)

Virtual presentation of abortion procedures (Life Dynamics, *LifeTalk* show on DVD, October, 2006)

Web Resources

www.abort73.com (Life Dynamics—site for youth)

www.afterabortion.org (Elliot Institute—post-abortion studies)

www.ehd.org (Endowment for Human Development—prenatal images)

www.hh76.com (Heritage House—all types of pro-life materials)

www.hli.org (Human Life International—international pro-life movement—see especially HLI's **"Pro-Life Talking Points"** series, one-page pro-life issue summaries downloadable on www.hli.org)

www.hopeafterabortion.com (Project Rachel—post-abortion counseling)

www.lifesitenews.com (Best, most comprehensive pro-life news source)

www.liveaction.org (Live Action—exposing Planned Parenthood)

www.internationaltaskforce.org (International Task Force on Euthanasia and Assisted Suicide—comprehensive resource on these subjects)

www.naprotechnology.com (also www.popepaulvi.com, Paul VI Institute for the Study of Human Reproduction, Omaha, NE—NaProTECHNOLOGY, moral infertility treatment)

www.ncbcenter.org (National Catholic Bioethics Center—bioethics and research)

www.rachelsvineyard.org (Rachel's Vineyard—post-abortion retreats)

www.vidahumana.org (*Vida Humana Internacional* - the most visited pro-life website in the Spanish language)

Ad Maiorem Dei Gloriam

About the Author

Rev. Thomas J. Euteneuer was born in Detroit, Michigan, in 1962, the fourth of seven children. He was ordained a priest in 1988 for the Diocese of Palm Beach, Florida and served in parishes in that diocese for twelve years before being given permission by his bishop to work full-time in pro-life ministry with Human Life International, where he has served as President since December of the year 2000.

Fr. Euteneuer has been performing exorcisms for seven years with approval from numerous dioceses in the United States. His interest in the ministry was a natural outgrowth of his work in the pro-life field, which deals with the organized power of evil on a global scale. Exorcism has allowed him to combine both his years of pastoral experience with his expertise in the pro-life movement. This book, *Demonic Abortion*, is the fruit of many years of prayer in front of abortion centers in the US and abroad and takes into account a very wide range of experiences that Fr. Euteneuer has had in confronting the culture of death on all five continents in more than a million miles of travel. Father offers the insights of this book as a means of forming and strengthening the Church Militant (a traditional term for the followers of Jesus Christ on earth). A strong Church Militant is the only sure hope of overcoming the evil practice of child sacrifice in the modern world.